Still Seeing

Bert Bell

1996

Bert Bell
Still Seeing Red
ISBN 0–906169–40–2

© Glasgow City Libraries and Archives 1996
Published by Glasgow City Libraries and Archives
Publications Board, The Mitchell Library, North Street, Glasgow G3 7DN

Front cover illustration Hi Hi Annual
The Hi Hi opening side for season 1948/49:–
Balunas, Orr, Petrie, Barclay, Kelly, Harrower.
Staroscik, Mason, Stirling, Ayton, Mitchell.

Back cover illustration
Author with ball used in Scottish Cup Final 1905
Thirds 3 Rangers 1

Contents

Dedication:

To my dear wife Nonagh, for her great patience, understanding, and encouragement, and in very fond memory of my constant Cathkin companion - DAD.

Acknowledgements:

My sincere thanks to all who have assisted me. My sons, Ian, Stuart, Alan and Gordon, who have helped in the research and gathering of memorabilia. Doug Baillie, and the Sunday Post, for access to their library and assistance. The Scottish Football League, Daily Record and The Sunday Mail, from whose pages have emanated information. Donald Cowey, Bobby Maitland and the late John Begg, from the fields of sports journalism. Former Thirds' players and club associates, D. Robertson and R. Laird of Glasgow. Press agencies whose files have provided other facets of Cathkin life.

Thanks also to the members of Glasgow City Libraries and Archives Publications Board, especially Verina Litster Commercial Manager, Margaret McBride graphic designer and Gerry Torley.

To Third Lanark fans worldwide in the USA, Canada, Portugal, Denmark, Australia, France, Italy, Spain, Germany, Hong Kong, the Republic of Ireland and Northern Ireland, from whom the author may have received and used material of interest.

Preface

The title was chosen to reflect the famous red shirts and also to acknowledge the wrath incumbent, even yet, in so many former Cathkin breasts, still feeling cheated by the sad demise of their club.

Although some 29 years have passed since its end, the Hi Hi have refused to accept a decent burial. Perhaps now, providing this historical review satisfies most, a final and proper farewell can be said.

The Thirds story has been written following extensive research, particularly because there were no club records available to the author. He has benefited greatly from the facts acquired from his own comprehensive collection of Third Lanark memorabilia. Personal visits have also been made to many former Cathkinites in an endeavour to ensure maximum accuracy, and factual anecdotes, which add the real Cathcart Road flavour to the contents.

The book is not necessarily a detailed account of every individual happening, but more an attempt to capture the moods, excitement, and atmosphere along with the football romance which prevailed in and around Cathkin for so many years.

It is intended for football fans in general and particularly for the thousands who so faithfully followed the fortunes of this once great wee club. It will recall the doubtful pleasure of sitting in the old grandstand which was for so long the butt of comedians' jokes throughout the land. It will envelop for as many, the terrific camaraderie and love for this institution, which was inherent in each Cathkin visit.

Third Lanark was all about people and the pleasure which the author derived in the preparation and compilation of this history, was only equalled by the almost embarrassing encouragement from his personal contacts in its pursuit.

There are still many 'steeped in red', who will feel that perhaps this chronicle is simply a warm wallow in nostalgia. We cannot forget, however, that to the real Cathkin man in the football sense what else is left for those **STILL SEEING RED?**

v

TRIBUTES TO THIRD LANARK

From all walks of life came the Hi Hi fans, to make their way to Cathkin Park each match day.

Several 'personalities', have taken the time and trouble to pen a few words of appreciation for the club, which provided them with much entertainment over the years.

The author was especially delighted with the flow of correspondence from former players, and notes from Adam McCulloch (1940s) and Dave Hilley (1960s) are included in these tributes.

Dear Bert,

"Come Away the Hi-Hi!" These words represent my early introduction to football as a young south-side-of-Glasgow boy, heard against a background of a noisy crowd, programme sellers and the ubiquitous vendors of macaroon bars and Spearmint chewing gum.

It is ironic that I now participate in this book about Third Lanark in my role as Chief Executive of the Scottish Football Association for I well remember the Saturday crowds making their way to Cathkin Park.

It would be fair to say that many still miss the habit of visiting the south side "match of the day" and as attitudes change, it is encouraging that you and others revive the interest in a famous old club sadly lost to the senior game.

Jim Farry - Chief Executive of the Scottish Football Association

Dear Mr. Bell,

As you will know, I helped to establish a little team called the Third Lanark Juveniles after the collapse of the senior club. We had a ground which I was able to secure off Holmlea Road and the club even had a visit to the United States to meet friends of Third Lanark and play against them.

All this showed I think that the superb spirit of Third Lanark was something which did not just die and I am sure there are many people in the south side of Glasgow who miss very much their visit to Cathkin.

I am delighted that you are writing the history because there must be many many thousands in Glasgow who will be overjoyed to read about the great days of such a fine team.

Sir Teddy Taylor, M.A., M.P. House of Commons, LONDON, SW1A 0AA

Dear Bert,

Many thanks for your letter regarding my spell at Cathkin, where I spent two years as manager. Let me add that perhaps I enjoyed my spell with the Thirds more than any other club I have been with. I was sad to move to Dundee when asked to do so, as at that time Thirds were one of the best teams in the league and were very popular with the crowds, both and home and away. It was a blow when they had to fold up.

Bob Shankly (Club Manager - 1957-1959)

Dear Bert,

Many thanks for your letter. I enclose two photographs taken in my dressing room at the Alhambra Theatre, Glasgow. I hope you will find them of some interest.

I have no data re. the Hi Hi that would be of much interest. I was in Australia when they folded and had sold my shares before I left, that was in 1962.

Like yourself, I miss the old team.

Good Luck frae, Alec Finlay

Bob Shankly and Alec Finlay were closely associated with Third Lanark and their tributes are worthy of inclusion although sadly both are now no longer with us.

Dear Bert,

The premature demise of Third Lanark AC in 1967 was a bitter blow to all who loved the Hi Hi. It was a tribute to their undying loyalty that the Supporters Club, including my father, continued to meet long after the last rites had been read, in the forlorn hope that a resurrection was imminent.

Sadly that was not to be, so all Thirds fans will be indebted to you for writing this book, to recall happy memories and ensure that the history of the famous old club is preserved for posterity

Dave Hilley

Dear Bert,

I was thrilled with all the data that you sent to my son, Andrew. It brought back wonderful memories of long ago, that neither time nor distance can obliterate.

Players like Jimmy Carabine, Jimmy Mason, Bobby Mitchell, Ayton, Mooney etc. etc., wonderful chaps and many a good laugh we had.

I still manage to kick the ball about with the young lads here; not much running involved but I can still show them a thing or two with the ball.

Adam McCulloch

Adam McCulloch 1945-1949.

CHAPTER 1

THE BEGINNING OF THE END ... AND THE BEGINNING.

The last day of season 1960/61 saw Third Lanark reach an historic landmark. They beat Hibernian 6-1 at Cathkin Park to reach a commendable 100 goals for the season, and their win secured an honourable third place in the most competitive first division league table.

The 'scarlet' goalscoring machine of Goodfellow, Hilley, Harley, Gray and McInnes had done it again. What price that strike-force in the market of the 1990s.

Only a short four years later the club's ultimate agony began. One dismal chapter of events followed another, until season 1965/66 found Thirds kicking off in the Second Division, having been relegated as a consequence of their most disastrous season ever, bringing the club only three wins from 34 matches in the league.

There followed yet another two seasons of mediocrity and discontent, ending in the humiliating defeat at Boghead Park when Dumbarton recorded a 5-1 score line, on Friday, 28th April, 1967. This game ended the soccer involvement of Thirds, as a senior professional club.

The following months brought a Board of Trade investigation, revealing constant player squabbles and bitter internal wrangles for power. These events finally took their toll and eventually a liquidator was appointed. Shortly after this move the dreaded announcement was made:

"THIRD LANARK WERE FINISHED"

The former glory chants of Hi Hi Hi became only memories, as the club had died of shame.

Subsequently, thousands of words have been penned to acknowledge the collapse. The Board of Trade enquiry report was sufficiently indicting to expose those responsible and these facts will be discussed later. Of course it is pertinent to highlight facets of neglect, but primarily the emphasis here will be centred around the tremendous contribution Third Lanark AC made to Scottish football during their glorious 95 years in existence.

We'll start at the beginning and join a truly valiant band of soldiers who met on 12th December, 1872, to form this once so proud club.

"Third Lanark: what romance surrounds that name. What glorious deeds the men in scarlet have achieved. The glamour which enfolds this club over the years, has grown whilst that of many others has diminished. From a very humble beginning Third Lanark, carefully watched over by men of wisdom and who have been indefatigable in their labours of love, has grown to be one of the most respected and powerful in the country. Proud traditions are here, traditions which will be worthily upheld in the days that face us ..."

These words were found in an historical booklet, produced by the club 60 years ago and which clearly identifies the objectives of the founders.

The first meeting of the club was held on 12th December, 1872, and had as its main objective "the forming of Third Lanark Rifle Volunteers as a football club, in affiliation to a most famous regiment of soldiers - The Third Lanark Rifle Volunteers".

The meeting had been called as a result of the original promoters attending the international match between Scotland and England at Hamilton Crescent. The gathering that evening in the Regimental Orderly room, of T.L.R.V. in Howard Street, Glasgow, was of one mind - to form a regimental club. The Scottish team of that day, in fact, included several military personnel from the Thirds - Billy Dickson, Billy McKinnon, Joe Taylor, to name but a few - and their inclusion particularly created this great interest. As it happened the international match which sparked all this off ended in a draw.

A certain Captain Inglis was elected first club president, and a committee then duly formed. The early recognition for organisation was given to John Wallace and Colonel John B Wilson. Wallace became Thirds first goalkeeper, and Wilson, playing in the now accepted striking role, scored

Thirds first ever league goal, which was reported at the time as an "epoch making score"...

It was decided at the first committee meeting that the annual subscription be 2/6, payable in advance. It was also resolved to apply for admission to the Football Association, as the SFA was not yet in existence.

A reproduction of the first minute is recorded below:

"How Third Lanark AC was born:"

The meeting had been duly advised by intimation of public notice. Private Broadfoot explained that it had been called for the purpose of organising if possible a football club, in connection with the TLRV regiment. He further confirmed that the Lieutenant Colonel, the majority of officers and 25 other ranks, had signified their willingness to support such a club. Sgt. Ralston then moved "That we the members now assembled should form ourselves into a club to be called Third LRV Football Club". This motion was seconded by Private Taylor, and gained unanimous approval. Private McKinnon proposed and Colour Sgt. Provan seconded, that Lt. Col. HE Crum-Ewing, be elected honorary president.

The uniform was discussed and it was agreed that it be - 1) A cowl - one end blue, the other yellow. 2) A scarlet guernsey. 3) Blue trousers or knickerbockers with blue stockings. A real colour ensemble. The next meeting agreed that on all guernseys the number 3 should be displayed.

The early minute carried several references to Queen's Park and, at the first AGM of March, 1873, a motion was carried that the members of that Club were also eligible to become office-bearers with Thirds.

The first playing field was on the old drill ground, at Victoria Road, Glasgow, just south of the regimental headquarters of the old TLRV, who latterly became the 7th Battalion the Cameronians (The Scottish Rifles).

The Scottish Cup was instituted in 1873, and the club gave their newly-formed side an opportunity to participate. The first reference in the minute book, called it the Scotland Cup. The "Redcoats" (the clubs original nickname from the scarlet uniform worn by the Third Lanark Rifle Volunteers) gallantly fought their way to the semi-final. Their displays enhanced the club's reputation so much that the following year, their right-back, John Hunter, became their first international cap winner when he was chosen to represent Scotland against England.

So rapidly did their fame grow, that many players were induced to pastures new. Queen's Park were the early vultures, swooping to take away Harry McNeill and John L Kaye. D Davidson followed to Hampden shortly afterwards.

In 1875 the powers realised that the original playing park surface was totally inadequate and poorly adapted for football. So rough was the surface that the committee decided it was unfair to ask clubs to play on it. Happily, and with the growing confidence of maturity, the executive decided to move to new headquarters. It was recorded in the minutes, that even this early in their career, The Warriors (another associated nickname with their origin) were becoming one of the best clubs in Scotland.

The new ground is what was latterly referred to as the Old Cathkin Park in Govanhill. It was the scene of many happy memories to older members, during the club's formative years. A minute of April, 1875 confirms that the secretary was instructed to call on "Dixons people"! (a renowned ironworks in Cathcart Road, Glasgow, who owned acres of land in the South-Side of the city) to ask if Thirds were at liberty to "fill up the furrows" on this most suitable piece of land. They received an affirmative and proceeded to complete the ground, including the erection of goal posts - with crossbars!

The prevailing enthusiasm became infectious and the membership increased dramatically. That same year a strange motion was put to the committee, regarding the club's name: "That it be changed to 'Glasgow Wanderers'"! Needless to say, it was soundly defeated and the proud Third Lanark Rifle Volunteers continued to perform. The season climaxed momentously when they lined up against already old rivals Queen's Park in the final of the Scottish Cup.

A creditable draw was fought against their more powerful opponents. In the replay, they lost 2-0, but at least found that their venture had been profitable. Indeed against Clydesdale at Cathkin in that tournament the gate money amounted to £10. 6.6. and, in a replay at Titwood, an additional £9.1/- was taken. More than a fair sum, over 100 years ago!

At the end of that season, the old Eastern club folded and Thirds were fortunate to purchase their best players. Amongst others were WS Somers and Sandy Kennedy. The former moved on again shortly to Queen's Park. Both players, however, figured prominently at Cathkin and also in Scotland's colours against the old enemy. Around this period Peter Andrews and JJ Lang donned the Scarlet.

Lang and Andrews claimed a couple of years later that they were the first Scots to be transferred south, when they joined Sheffield Wednesday.

Having reached the cup finals of 1875 and '76, without the aid of their newly-acquired talent, it was confidently expected that they would go one better in '77 and capture the trophy. No such luck, as they were drawn against the redoubtable Vale of Leven and went down 1-0. The club regularly reached cup finals, but sadly they remained the bridesmaid.

Another tournament began in 1877, with the arrival of the Glasgow Charity Cup.

Thirds had struggled for this handsome trophy for a few years before finding themselves in the final of 1884. Alas, they again ran out losers to Queen's Park.

Cathkin's first grandstand was erected in 1878. The cost was £155. The contractors chose (even then) to take half of each gate drawings until the account was paid in full. What vision ...

Cathkin was chosen as the venue for the international match against England, and the association hastily erected a temporary stand opposite the grandstand. The ground was regularly used for all Charity Cup matches during that season.

5

Thirds remained out of the limelight for the next four years, but used this fallow spell to build up a good side. Season 1888/89 brought with it extremely high hopes for success and so it proved. Indeed this was to become the most outstanding season to date in the club's history.

In the national cup there was neither a qualifying sector or a seeded draw. Every club went into the hat and the winners could certainly lay claim to being the best. Thirds duly accomplished this feat in grand style. They played no fewer than 13 games in eight rounds and were the first team to undergo such a severe test. Of all the gripping struggles endured, surely the finest was against Celtic in what went down in history as the "snow final".

When the clubs arrived at Hampden for the game, they found one of the largest attendances seen up to that time. Unfortunately, they also found that the snow was ankle deep on the pitch.

The consensus appeared to accept that the ground was not playable, but the referee proceeded with the match. In a gruelling and, in the circumstances, fast match, Thirds registered an excellent 3-0 win.

Post-match activity, not surprisingly, centred around a strong protest from Celtic. A special meeting was called by the SFA, and referee Charles Campbell and umpires RF Harrison and FR Park were also asked to attend. After some deliberation, a replay was ordered to take place the following week. This time the Hi Hi endorsed their early promise with a great 2-1 victory, to take the trophy for the first time. The origins of the nickname "Hi Hi" have been many and varied. In fact the cry came about as a consequence of a band of fans making mock reference to a Thirds' defender's clearance during an early league match, as the ball was belted 'high high' out of the ground. Thereafter Hi Hi became synonymous with the club.

As a consequence of this win, the demand for Thirds' players increased. Several transfers followed and they became a rather weakened side. However, Thirds won the Charity Cup again in 1890, to keep the fans in good heart. The Scottish Football League was born in 1890 and they became automatically founder members. Their first representative to the league was John Thomson, honorary secretary of the club.

Memory Picture—This is the Third Lanark team which won the Charity Cup in season 1889-90. ©Hi Hi Annuals.

7

It was from that year that Thirds appeared in the more familiar red and white colours. The shirts were red with white vertical stripes, and the shorts remained black.

A financial crisis arrived mid-1893, but the club moved instantly to ensure stability. A levy of £1 per head per member, brought sufficient returns to keep them afloat. Once again in 1897/98, the Charity Cup was won.

Came the dawn of the present century, and with it a second classical period. They had now reverted to the long accepted colour scheme of red jerseys and white pants, dispensing with the cowl.

Former Cathkin favourite Hugh Wilson, who had gone to Sunderland, had expressed a desire to return north. Hugh was now supposed to be well past his best and was playing in Bristol. Thirds risked the wrath of all and paid a handsome transfer fee of £50 to bring him home and begin a new era at Cathkin.

The first match against Hibernian would decide the inter city championship. With Wilson's outstanding influence, Thirds took the honours, and followed this by winning the Charity Cup in the Exhibition Stadium, beating Celtic 3-0 after a goal less draw.

It is worth noting that the club's levy of £1 per head, had now been repaid in full.

The arrival of another bunch of characters, including McIntosh, Maxwell, Neilson, Graham, McKenzie, Campbell, Wardrope, Prior, Comrie and Munro, further consolidated the playing staff and retained the club's prominence, which enabled them, during the early years of this century, to ensure further celebrations.

The Glasgow Cup was won for the first time in 1902/03 and the League Championship came in 1903/04, along with the retention of the Glasgow Cup. It was also in 1903/04 that Third Lanark became a limited liability company.

Winning the league was a remarkable feat, considering that all home games were played 'away' at either Hampden or elsewhere, due to the club's plans to move to a new home which was not quite ready.

©*Supplement to Ideas. 1903/04 1st Division Champions*
E.M. Tabbat, T. Sloan, R. Ferguson, J. Brownlie, J.A. Dickson, J. Cross, R. Barr,
J. Campbell, T. Fairfoull, J. Kidd, J. McFie, A.M. Ballantine, D.A. Hill, W. McIntosh,
J. Richardson, J. Johnstone, R. Hosie.

The Scottish Cup again found its way to Cathkin when Thirds beat Rangers 3-1 in a stirring final, in addition to taking home the Glasgow League Championship and Second XI Cup. Happy days were certainly back at Cathkin Park.

The following season, the Glasgow League Championship was again won, but Thirds were knocked out of the Scottish and Glasgow Cups at the final hurdle.

Obviously some of the Cathkin stars were growing older and this along with transfers, resulted in a much leaner time being experienced for almost three more seasons.

Rob Barr, Member of Side - Note Striped Jersey. ©Pillans & Crawford.

Every cloud has a silver lining, however, and for Thirds theirs came in the shape of the signing of a youngster called Jimmy Brownlie, who was to become arguably the most famous goalkeeper in the history of the game. Fuller details will appear later on Brownlie, but suffice to say now that, immediately on arrival, he became involved in a quite incredible series of Glasgow Cup games. They won the cup, but it took them an amazing 10 games to complete the tournament. Indeed, one of the most amusing incidents ever recorded took place in the final against Celtic.

"Tod" Sloan of Thirds put his foot clean through the ball, in the act of clearing, a hitherto unheard-of occurrence. It took three games to dispose of Partick Thistle, four games to see off Clyde and another three against Celtic in the final, before ultimate victory. That record-breaking side was: Brownlie; Sloan, Hill; Fairfoul, Ferguson, McIntosh; Johnston, Hosie, Richardson, McFie and Cross.

Thirds v Kilmarnock 1911. Hosie Heading into the Kilmarnock Goal. ©Mirror of Life.

Team building continued assiduously until around season 1913/14 when a most competent side had been formed. They reached the final of the Glasgow Cup and semi-final of the Scottish. The company was now well in funds and a dividend had been paid. The next season appeared full of promise until circumstances altered events. World War I was declared and most of the Thirds players, like true volunteers, enlisted immediately.

Some made the supreme sacrifice, with others, for different reasons, unable to play the game again. Thirds carried on during hostilities in common with others and performed reasonably well in the Southern league.

The First World War statistics show:

Season	P	W	D	L	F	A	Pts	DIV	Posn
1914/15	38	10	12	16	51	57	32	A	16
1915/16	38	9	11	18	38	56	29	SL	17
1916/17	38	19	11	8	53	37	49	SL	5
1917/18	34	10	7	17	56	62	27	SL	13
1918/19	34	11	9	14	60	60	31	SL	12

Survival would best describe the trend then rather than a high level of performance.

On return to normality, Thirds again proved that on their day they could match the best, but found themselves still short of championship form.

Season 1919/20, became boom time in Scottish football with huge crowds flocking back to watch their favourites. Thirds resumed under the chairmanship of Col. Wilson, and the nucleus of their side included Brownlie, McCormick, Orr and Lennon.

Thirds - 1921
Caldwell, Findlay, Walker, Muir, Jarvie, McCormack, McLaughlin, McInally, Hillhouse, Christie, Reid, Orr, Walker, McKenna, Higgins, Brown ©"Pals".

The next three years were difficult and, in 1922, the jubilee was celebrated quietly. The first 50 years had come and gone. Their league position was ninth, but no cup success was forthcoming that season to mark their first 50 years.

Unfortunately, the warning signs were ignored in 1924/25. Thirds were ultimately punished severely. At the half way stage of the season, they were sitting proudly in fourth top spot, but to the horror of all a series of dreadful results brought relegation for the first time and they dropped into the second division. Fittingly, it was recorded in the minutes that whilst it may be invidious to mention individual names of the playing culprits it must be noted that the relegated side contained a fair number of international players - which said it all.

Bill Findlay, Sam Brown, John Jarvie, Walter Frame, Tom Williamson, Tom McInally, Alec Reid, Jas. Walker, John McCormack, Frank Walker, Bobby Archibald.

Three weary seasons found Thirds operating in the lower regions but at last they returned to the first division. This was really a case of flattering only to deceive because they dropped again the following campaign. This time the duration of exile was short and ended with them winning the Second Division Championship in 1931. They had scored an incredible 107 league goals, an achievement which they never bettered during their lifetime in football.

Second Division Champions-1931
Moreland, J. Clark, Simpson, Waugh, Warden, McLellan, Lynas, Jack, Dewar, Blair, Breslin.

The Cathkin complexion assumed a much rosier hue over the next three seasons, although great was the disappointment when they were again relegated at the end of season 1933/34. It was for one season only and they returned to the top league with the league flag flying proudly to celebrate their winning the second division.

The years 1931-36 saw the introduction of a new fixed policy for the club. This effectively provided a good measure of stability. Under the chairmanship of James M Milne and with the full backing of the board, it was decided that, with the aim of building a team worthy of the name, there must be no transfers. The policy was firmly adhered to and, despite many tempting offers from other clubs, refusals were the order of the day. Tom Jennings, the incumbent of the manager's chair, was to be encouraged in every possible way to provide a successful side.

The season 1935-36 ended with Thirds in a safe position in the league and looking forward to taking part in the Scottish Cup final against Rangers at Hampden in May.

Despite what was acknowledged to be a tremendous contribution by Thirds on the day, the cup went to Ibrox. A defensive slip early in the game allowed Rangers to score the solitary goal and a combination of careless finishing and superb goalkeeping from Jerry Dawson, ensured that Thirds' efforts were nullified. Full details of this match will appear in a later chapter.

The cream of the previous season's playing crop was still available in the

new campaign 1936/37 and included many names to conjure up cup and glory dreams for the faithful: Muir, Hall, Carabine, Harvey, Rhodie, Johnston, Blair, Craig, Black, McInnes, Morrison, Jones, Yardley, Hay, Sharpe, Milne, McCaskill, McMillan, Denmark, Kennedy.

Geordie Hay was top scorer with 17 goals, closely followed by Kennedy on 16. McInnes made the most appearances with a superb 38 and was chased for this honour in consistency by Jimmy Denmark and Carabine, on 37 each.

Father Time and transfer activity wrought havoc on the side in season 1937/38. Skipper Denmark moved to Newcastle United, McMillan went to Cardiff, Hay to Queen of the South and Milne and Sharpe chose the colours of Bournemouth and Derry City respectively.

Jimmy Denmark – A Cathkin Favourite. ©Hi Hi Annual.

Their departures were well compensated for by the return of Neilly Dewar to the fold, from Sheffield. He was seen as the perfect foil to bring on the then relatively unknown Jimmy Mason. Speaking of Mason, as he frequently did in football company, former Rangers and Scotland internationalist Willie Waddell, said "Aye, wee Jimmy was quite the finest inside man, I ever played with. He always knew where to find you with the ball and his accuracy and defence-splitting passes, made a winger's life so much easier." Quite an accolade from a Scotland great.

Back to Cathkin, and mid-table respectability was the reward for reasonable effort. More importantly, sufficient potential had been seen within the playing ranks to ensure that the faithful returned in large numbers the following season.

Statistics showed that the leading scorer was the returned exile Neilly

Dewar with 18, Kennedy again proving he knew the road to goal with 15. Jimmy Blair's consistency was apparent with 38 appearances, with Dewar close behind on 35.

Signed players for the new 1938/39 season were: Goalkeepers: McCaffrey and Muir. Backs: Carabine, McCulloch, Johnston, Smith. Half-backs: Black, Barr, Sowerby, Simpson, McLellan. Forwards: Hart, Mason, Dewar, Wilson, Kennedy, Jones, Kinnaird, and Watters. A prominent name missing was that of Jimmy Blair, who had refused initial terms. Later in the season this Cathkin favourite returned to the fold and again played his part for the Hi Hi.

Archie Hart – Formed a devasting Right Wing Partnership with Jimmy Mason during the late Thirties. ©Scottish Football Book.

The season, at best, was indifferent. Thirds managed to prevent

15

opposing forwards from scoring 100 goals ... just! They lost 96. The redeeming feature was the fact that they scored 80 during the season. At one stage the team's position gave some cause for concern and, although they performed well on occasions, the lack of consistent fire power cost them dearly. Clyde knocked Thirds out of the Scottish Cup in round four. Rangers narrowly defeated them by seven corners to three in the Charity Cup final, to prove conclusively it was not a Hi Hi year. On a happy note, Dewar was again leading scorer with 31, although newcomer "Soldier" Jones chased him all the way with 27. There were few complaints when the season's curtain fell, with all anticipating the next. However, a certain Mr Hitler had other ideas and war was declared on 3rd September, 1939. This changed quite dramatically the football scene over the next six years.

The handbook for the pre-war season reveals several interesting facts. George McMillan had succeeded Tom Jennings as manager. A total of 34 players from Thirds had been capped over the years and the following full list of honours achieved during their first 50 years, was extremely encouraging.

Thirds had won the First Division Championship in 1903/04 and had twice been Second Division champions in 1930/31 and 1934/35.

The Scottish Cup was won in 1888/89 and again in 1904/05.

In 1900/01 they took the Inter-City Championship trophy, and they added the Glasgow League title in 1904/05 and 1905/06.

Having been involved in nine Glasgow Cup finals, they went on to win that trophy in 1902/03, 1903/04 and 1908/09.

The handsome Glasgow Charity Cup had adorned the Cathkin trophy cabinet in 1889/90, 1897/98 and 1900/01.

To this point, therefore, Third Lanark had won every single honour available to a Glasgow club but, despite these awards, the spectre of debt remained and, at the end of season 1938/39, Thirds reported a loss of £2,399 with Rangers and Celtic showing profits of £7,082 and £4,415 respectively. "Twas ever thus ..."

CHAPTER 2

SEASONAL TRENDS

When war was declared on 3rd September, 1939, the football season was in full swing and five games had been played in Division A.

The Scottish Football League then called a halt to proceedings, to give themselves time to consider the implications.

On 4th September, the SFA advised all affiliated clubs that the government had banned any gathering of crowds, decreeing that such events would present a real target for the enemy. It would not be practical in their opinion to allow such assemblies.

Players' contracts were cancelled, although their registrations with clubs remained in force. Daily discussions were taking place between the government and the prevailing football powers to reach an acceptable alternative. It was recognised that there would be some benefit to be gained from distracting peoples' minds from the on-going severe stresses and tensions of war.

Mid-September arrived and the Home Secretary gave permission for some friendly games to take place but only in "neutral zones". The areas chosen included Glasgow, Edinburgh, Dundee, Dunfermline and Clydebank. There followed a ban, then, on competitive games and, as a consequence, the Scottish League Management Committee officially abandoned the 1939/40 league competitions.

Following pleas from all quarters, the viability of "regional leagues" was discussed and clubs were asked for their views. This ultimately led to a mini resumption of football, with competitive matches being allowed, following the Scottish Secretary's declaration on 21st September, 1939. Crowd restrictions were hastily applied as follows:

Ibrox, Hampden and Parkhead - maximum 15,000; with all other grounds limited to 8,000. Friendlies were promptly arranged on an interim basis and Thirds had a good win against Queen's Park at Hampden 4-3 in one such match.

Agreement was finally reached for the resumption of full competitive activity under the new regional league basis, which helped considerably with travelling problems.

Thirds were put into the South and West League, along with Motherwell, Clyde, Albion Rovers, Morton, Kilmarnock, Celtic, Partick Thistle, St Mirren, Queen's Park, Ayr United, Airdrie, Dumbarton, Rangers, Queen of South and Hamilton Academical.

This was the compilation of clubs for the first war-time season. Further discussions eventually led to the birth of the Southern League, for the duration of hostilities. The following clubs became members:

Airdrie, Albion Rovers, Celtic, Clyde, Dumbarton, Falkirk, Motherwell, Partick Thistle, Queen's Park, Rangers, St Mirren, Thirds, Hibernian, Hearts, Hamilton Academical and Morton.

Back now to the first war-time season and, when the original A Division was scrapped, Thirds had accumulated five points. They had beaten Cowdenbeath and Kilmarnock 4-2 and 1-0 respectively and drawn with Hamilton Academical.

All clubs were then faced with the problems of player availability and were allowed to play "guests" for convenience and also with the blessing of the SFA. Thirds' war time record is again one of survival and the undernoted chart will serve to support this and remind readers of a few greats to play in scarlet at that time:

Season	League Points	Leading Scorer	Goals Scored
1939/40	30	Neilly Dewar	11
1940/41	25	Jack Jones	13
1941/42	33	Johnny Connor	27
1942/43	20	Johnny Connor	21
1943/44	17	George Henderson	24
1944/45	24	Kenny Dawson	14
1945/46	26	Kenny Dawson	13

An interesting introduction to a match report on the Thirds v Rangers game at Ibrox, on Saturday, 7th October, 1939, was carried in a Glasgow evening sports paper. As usual at this time, club announcers reminded all attending of the current air raid instructions and on this occasion the journalist introduced his "piece" by saying: "The guy who issued the air raid instructions prior to this match has a lot to answer for. This 90 minutes had us all forgetting the war and the only air raids were those created by Waddell and Thornton at one end and Jones, Hart and Dewar at the other." This with reference to a thrilling 2-2 draw.

When the curtain came down on this first war time season, Thirds were fifth bottom of the league, but already it was evident that the vagaries of player availability would determine the club's future playing fortunes during hostilities.

Neilly Dewar topped the Cathkin scoring charts with 11 goals. He was closely chased by "Soldier" Jones with nine. Jones, of course, went on to become a real Hi Hi hit man with his unselfish play, dribbling skills and powerful shot.

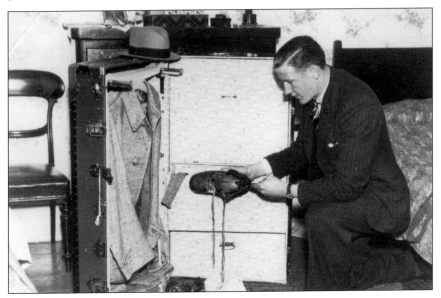

Jack "Soldier" Jones – Packing for SFA Tour of Canada & USA, 1939.

Season 1940/41 was the first campaign under the Southern League banner with Hibernian, Hearts and Falkirk replacing Ayr United, Kilmarnock and Queen of the South. The following men wore the scarlet against Morton in the opener: McCaffrey; Stewart, T Black; Blair, Woodburn, Sinclair; Watters (Cowdenbeath), Proudfoot, Dewar, Jones, Stevenson.

Inconsistency was again the campaign keynote. A solitary double against Airdrie and an excellent Ibrox victory was quickly negated by scorelines like Albion Rovers 6 Thirds 1.

It took Thirds eight consecutive matches to grab their first point, in a draw at Shawfield, on 28th September. Three weeks later came the first win bonus against Airdrie, 3-2.

Jones was top scorer with 13. At this time Tom Bayne (Brentford), Glancy (Portsmouth) and Kenny Dawson (Falkirk) all guested for Thirds, with Dawson wearing the colours on four occasions.

A warm welcome to Cathkin was given to a little "big" man, in the scoring sense. Johnny Connor arrived and quickly became an instant hit with the fans.

Giant defender Willie Watson from Ashfield completed this little-and-large duo and it did not take him long to stamp his authority on things.

October, 1940 found director Willie Campbell donning the managerial mantle for a short spell.

A spell of extremely low temperatures around December/January led to a plea from director Campbell for "gloves for the players" on the morning of the match against Rangers on 5th January, 1941.

The local police constabulary came to the rescue and supplied the whole team with the necessary hand warmers. Warm hands, however, did not prevent Rangers winning by the odd goal, Thirds again paying the penalty against the Light Blues.

It may come as a surprise to some but Thirds were on the verge of signing the one and only Billy Steel, prior to his becoming a Morton player. On

24th May, 1941, director Campbell received the following telegram from Steel following hush-hush negotiations: "Sorry can't play for you next week signed for Morton today!"

All Scottish fans will remember those two little maestros Steel and Mason display their repertoire of skills in the colours of Scotland in 1948. What would an identikit job seven years earlier in club colours have meant to Thirds fans?

A rather amusing incident occurred on Saturday, 22nd February, 1941, as Thirds prepared to line up against Celtic at Parkhead, as a consequence of some misunderstanding between player Hall and the directors. Two weeks earlier, Thirds had signed Henry Hall from Ayr, after the regular Cathkin 'keeper, McCaffrey, had been injured. Hall, therefore, was called to play at Parkhead. On his arrival, he reminded the Thirds board of their promise of a signing-on fee which had not materialised. The board chose to ignore his request, directed Hall to a stand seat and instructed the injured McCaffrey to take up his usual place. Thirds lost this match 4-3!

The fans were not unduly sorry to wave goodbye to this campaign but, ever the optimists, they even looked forward to the next.

Not one but a series of new brooms had arrived at Cathkin in season 1941/42 during the break, in the hope of sweeping up some honours.

These comments referred to the appointment of three new directors and six new signings.

There followed a board statement which said: "We are going all out for long-awaited success and no expense will be spared in its achievement."

The opening XI will provide early evidence of the personnel changes: Wylie; Carabine, Rennie; Stevenson, Watson, Kelly; Park, Glancey, Connor, Jones, Hughes.

The scoring exploits of Johnny Connor quickly became the icing on the Thirds cake. No question but his 27 strikes helped the Hi Hi climb to a very respectable sixth league place.

Bobby Mitchell, 1947. ©Hi Hi Annual.

Some interesting league results were mixed with a disappointing lack of cup consistency.

League doubles against Dumbarton, Hearts and Airdrie delighted the locals, but the sheer embarrassment of losing 13 goals cumulatively to Hibernian in the Summer Cup brought all back to earth with a bang.

Problems arose also with the arrival of the Summer Cup. Season tickets were not acceptable because this competition was run outwith the deadline of 30th April. Due to complete lack of communication, fans were enraged to learn of this at the eleventh hour but, following protracted and heated discussion, people power prevailed and season tickets were accepted.

In Season 1942/43, eight wins and four draws from 30 league games left a lot to be desired. Thirds finished the season in fourth bottom spot. They defeated Queen's Park both home and away which allowed the die-hards to release some tension.

The unexpected bonus in this campaign came with the arrival of Bobby "Twinkle Toes" Mitchell, who made his debut on Saturday, 9th August. Despite his electrifying wing runs, Mitchell could not prevent a first class Clyde team from winning.

Mitchell starred in this side against the Bully Wee.

McCaffrey; Watson, Rennie; Blair; Black, Sinclair; Fraser, Jones, Connor, McGill, Mitchell.

On Saturday, 17th December, 1942, a little piece of Cathkin history was made off the field.

Former Thirds and Scotland goalkeeper, Jimmy Brownlie (star of the early 1900s), returned his 11 Scottish international jerseys to the SFA for safe-keeping.

It was the practice during Brownlie's playing days for the SFA to provide their goalkeeper with the identical jersey as the remainder of the squad.

If the recipient wished to wear "additionally", a sweater, then he had to buy that himself.

Reaching the semi-final of the Southern League Cup was their biggest day for about six years but the Hi Hi were well beaten by Falkirk 3-1.

The Thirds side was: McBride; Carabine, Rennie; Blair, Currie, Kelly; Jess, Fraser, Connor, Jones, Cairns. Carabine scored Thirds' consolation in the 80th minute.

Towards the end of this season, Thirds faced Celtic in the final of the Glasgow Charity Cup. A combination of nerves, defensive errors and a complete lack of the finishing touch gave Celtic a sound 3-0 win.

In the space of three weeks Thirds had been knocked out of two cup competitions, which had the faithful again pondering on the future.

Season 1943/44 was Thirds' worst war-time campaign. There was fortunately no relegation and that saved the day, as they plummeted to the league basement with only seven wins and three draws to their credit.

One point only from six League Cup games at the season's back end and a first-round knock-out in the Summer Cup did not please.

An event in itself was their reaching the final of the Glasgow Cup, but Partick Thistle defused their spark with a 4-2 win.

The season of discontent ultimately led to a fans' revolt and demonstration against the board and their policies. This took place on 4th March, 1944, prior to the League Cup opener against Hibernian. The fans claimed that there was clearly an attitude of indifference and apathy at board level and frustration was further increased when a board decision led to the very popular Connor being allowed to leave the club.

Inevitably, much dirty linen was exposed and the directors were again encouraged to "resign en bloc".

A hastily-arranged board meeting took place the following week and it was subsequently announced publicly that Thirds would not be allowed to languish further and, that immediate steps would be taken to prepare for the future.

On 2nd October, 1943, keeper Roy Henderson made his debut for Thirds against Hamilton at Cathkin and, whilst finishing on the losing side, did enough to indicate that the club had made a fine capture.

An amazing match took place at Brockville on Saturday, 30th October. The scoreline was remarkable in itself (6-5 for Thirds) but even that took second place to the most clinical scoring touch seen in years. It came from Thirds' mystery striker who hit four excellent goals with Mason and Jones making it six.

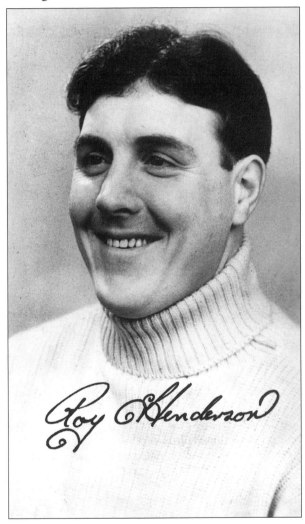

Roy Henderson. ©Evening Citizen.

The "Newman" was soon identified as George Henderson, brother of Roy. This character provided the fire power over the next three seasons, to help the fans forget Connor.

One of the finest men ever in scarlet appeared in the side which won at Brockville. He was a man who, over the next 13 seasons, gave his all for the Cathkin cause. Harry Mooney, quickly to be tagged "The Iron Man" had arrived.

An SFA announcement regarding prices for future international games at Hampden Park was made at this time.

25

Centre stand seats would now cost £1.10/-, with others ranging from £1.1/, down to terracing briefs at 2/6d.

An appeal by Thirds for clothing coupons, to buy new playing kits, was made prior to the game against Airdrie on 7th November. Any surplus coupons held by fans would be greatly appreciated. This request was met in full from a most unexpected source which will be revealed later.

A campaign of mediocrity ended and on this occasion there was more concern than hope, in anticipation.

Season 1944/45 was also poor in most respects. A final league place of fourth bottom was not surprising as only nine wins were recorded.

George McMillan had returned to the manager's chair and this appointment, given time, was looked on as a move to stabilise the club.

Thirds had swooped on Hampden during the summer and signed Bowman, Aitken and Cox to bolster their defence, although their national service duties restricted regular appearances.

Willie Barclay arrived on the scene and this defender soon displayed his prodigious work rate and skilful defending techniques.

Two ex-Ibrox favourites completed the signing spree. Willie McIntosh and veteran Bobby Bolt moved across the city to wear the scarlet. Quite an injection of experience and youth.

A couple of months later Kenny Dawson, the man with dynamite in his boots, joined them and fast became a fan's favourite. Kenny went further and took the Cathkin scoring honours over the next two seasons with 14 and 13 goals respectively.

Thirds plans were badly hit early in the season when McIntosh broke his leg in a game against Hamilton, although to help offset this the Harrower brothers arrived mid-season and both Jimmy and Billy played their part in the mini-revival.

On 26th May, 1945, in the Summer Cup opener against Falkirk, the Thirds XI was: McBride; Kelly, J Harrower; Bolt, Black, Ashe; McIntosh, Guy, Henderson, W Harrower and Dawson.

A 2-1 win against the Bairns was pleasing but soon forgotten as Thirds went down in the return leg tie, 5-0.

Three good league results included the double over Thistle and a magnificent 6-4 defeat of Motherwell at Fir Park. Rangers, as had been their habit, ended Thirds' further interest in the League Cup, with Falkirk doing similarly in the summer edition.

Hope springs eternal in the Cathkin breast and this was never more necessary than now, to ensure some sort of support for the next season.

A change in league structure was brought into being, in season 1945/46. The Scottish Football League re-opened all competitions on a geographical basis. A & B Leagues were formed and Thirds found themselves placed with the elite in A Division.

Some new faces appeared at Cathkin. Alex Venters (Rangers) and Archie Coates (Dundee) came in, whilst Andy McGill took the return ticket to Hampden.

Kenny Dawson. ©Topical Times.

The sequel to the previous season's plea for clothing coupons arrived out of the blue in the shape of several giant parcels from Argentine. Yes, Thirds had apparently been well remembered from their Tour of 1923 and, amazingly, their pleas had reached these foreign shores, with the outcome of a brand new playing strip and two match balls being sent by the Argentinian FA.

Thirds wore the strip for the first time in their game against Motherwell, at Fir Park and duly celebrated with a 3-1 victory!

Many readers will recall that, on the insistence of the SFL, all clubs were obliged to play on both Christmas and Boxing Day and 1st/2nd January,

A unique photo of Cathkin Park, 1950 – Well Packed

providing no Sundays were involved in these dates. Bearing in mind that there could also be the "odd" normal Saturday fixture to fit in, it was not unusual to watch your club, home and away, on five or six occasions, weather permitting, during a 14-day festive spell.

Midway through this campaign the Thirds team most frequently was: Petrie; Carabine, Kelly; Bolt, Harrower, Sinclair; Lister, Coates, McCulloch, Venters; Dawson.

Alex Venters made his debut against Motherwell at Cathkin and his first goals for the club came in the League Cup game against Queen's Park. Indeed Venters notched a double just three weeks after signing on.

Ian McBride and Roy Henderson, two excellent keepers, were allowed to depart. Thirds chose to hold on to the tried and well-tested Petrie, Fraser and Bayne.

In May a further two signings indicated some determination to add experience and guile to the team and Dave Kinnear from Rangers, together with George Merchant from Aberdeen, were welcomed to the fold.

28

John Petrie. ©Hi Hi Annual.

An extremely ambitious attempt by Thirds to obtain the services of Stanley Matthews for the game against Rangers, in the Charity Cup final, failed. The Ibrox boys won this game which drew a massive crowd of 48,700.

All clubs were reminded that, on 30th April, wartime players' contracts expired and this resulted in feverish activity to secure new agreements with the players each club wished to retain.

Thirds completed their league activity in a more respectable mid-table place, which gave the fans hope of improvement come August.

Normality returned in full to the Scottish football scene in season 1946/47 and Thirds kicked off all home games at neighbours Queen's Park ground at Hampden, due to reconstruction work still being carried out at Cathkin.

The following side faced Aberdeen at Pittodrie, on Saturday, 10th August: Petrie; Balunas, Kelly; Bolt, Black, Sinclair; Henderson, Mason, McCulloch, Venters, Kinnaird. Aberdeen registered a comfortable 3-0 win.

Line up v Celtic 4/9/46
Carabine, Kelly, Petrie, Bolt, Palmer, Mooney, McCulloch, Ayton, Henderson, Venters, Mitchell.

The Cathkin boys did not record a win until 4th September when they defeated Celtic. Thirds reversed an interval deficit with goals from Henderson (2), Venters and Mitchell, making it a fine 4-1 victory. The team was: Petrie: Carabine, Kelly: Bolt, Barclay, Mooney: McCulloch, Ayton, Henderson, Venters, Mitchell.

The 9th of November signalled the start of a revival when the Hi Hi beat Falkirk 4-2. With only two exceptions, Thirds went on to win every match up to and including the Scottish Cup replay against Hamilton.

The real find of this season was young centre-half Alex Palmer, who surprised more than a few when he was chosen as Cathkin's Player of the Year. To do that he had to outpoint such as Mooney, Mason and Mitchell, and that was recognised as a first-class achievement.

Mitchell and Mason both distinguished themselves in the colours of Scotland when they were selected to play for the league side against their English counterparts at Hampden. In some ways they were unfortunate to be in a side which virtually crumpled against some brilliant English forward play, but both lads performed admirably and were well worth their further consideration.

Respectability only in the league, bottom place in the League Cup section and a shock dismissal from the Scottish Cup by Dumbarton, presented a real sorry tale of woe.

In Season 1947/48, Cathkin diehard Jimmy Carabine completed his first full term in charge of team affairs but he could not look back with total satisfaction.

Eleventh league place, another k.o. in the Scottish Cup at Motherwell and no success in the League Cup.

Rangers and Celtic respectively ended Thirds' interest in the Glasgow and Charity Cups.

An impressive double in the league over Celtic and Hearts was rendered less satisfying by them being the recipients of similar treatment from Dundee, Hibernian, Motherwell, Rangers and St. Mirren.

"Looking for Inspiration". Thirds Party at Brora 27/2/48. ©Caithness Studios.
Petrie, Brora Player, Good, Bogan, Balunas, Brora Player, Mason, Scott, Orr, Kelly,
Mooney, Brora Official, Bailey San Uncles.

The highest-scoring games for the Warriors were against Celtic and Queen of the South when Thirds netted five each time. But again the memory fades when lined up against the Falkirk and Hibernian defeats of 8-1 and 8-0.

The financial constraints resulted in team building being of the "bargain basement" variety, although despite this there arrived at Cathkin a player from Poland, Feliks Staroscik, who lit up many dark Cathkin moments with a scintillating brand of wing play and devastating shot.

Thirds' first Australian player also joined up. Goalkeeper Bill Fraser arrived with an excellent pedigree and doubters were not left long in that state, as Bill earned the respect of all with his enthusiasm, attitude and competent displays.

Jim Young, from Beith Juniors, received an early introduction to the first team when he was called to replace the injured Matt Balunas and a series of first-class displays quickly endeared him to the fans.

"Starry" on left – A nippy thrustful winger with a powerful shot. ©Hi Hi Annual.

Controversy surrounded Thirds' exit from the Scottish Cup. The club had in fact protested prior to the start of the tie against Motherwell that the Fir Park keeper's jersey was extremely similar in colour to that of the outfield players, but their complaint carried no weight and the match went ahead.

The 'Well opened their account early and there was no dispute about the goal. A problem arose late in the second half when Thirds were denied by what they saw as blatant handball by a defender. The referee thought otherwise, convinced that the keeper had handled the ball. Motherwell celebrated the let-off by scoring a second.

Further Cathkin protests were in vain, although in fairness the ineffectiveness of their forwards on the day made the task difficult outwith complaints about refereeing decisions.

On Christmas Day 1947 the Thirds rejoicing was great as the fans trekked back to watch their favourites in the familiar surroundings of Cathkin Park.

For the first time in 18 months, Thirds trotted out at "home" to face Aberdeen in a league match. A 3-1 win was the start of yet another "Houdini act", which found them leaping to safety from the league basement. Jimmy Carabine deserved his share of plaudits for the revival, having shown tremendous faith in several of the squad by persisting with them.

Thirds – December 1947. Back Stage at Alhambra Theatre Glasgow with Hi Hi Fan wee Alec Finlay. ©Evening Citizen.
This Group includes Staroscik, Mason, Balunas, Harrower, Orr, Christie, Mooney, Cuthbertson, Henderson.

The team showed a few changes in season 1948/49 but left the fans asking: "Can the forwards find more finishing power?" Last season the Mitchell left foot was about the only real weapon in the armoury, although Staroscik showed promise of becoming a super snapper of chances, given the support.

Newcomers Smith (ex Hearts), Thom (Hew McGowan Vics) and Crawford (Vale of Leven) all joined up to complete the following pool:

34

Ayton, Barclay, Balunas, Bogan, Baillie, Christie, Cameron, Dewar, Fraser, Harrower, Kelly, McCulloch, Mason, Middleton, Myles, Bobby Mitchell, Alex McLeod, Robert Mitchell, Orr, Petrie, Reid, Scott, Stirling, Staroscik, Young and Henderson.

Norman Christie, Alex McLeod, Alan Orr also known as Messrs. Poise, Power & Polish. ©*Caithness Studios.*

"Bobby" Mitchell went on to great fame with Newcastle United whilst "Robert" did not appear to be given much opportunity at this time to break through.

Much as usual was expected of maestro Mason, but this play-making general was the provider of chances and still needed the clinical finishing skills of others in support.

Roles reversed. Comedian Alec Finlay signs on for Jimmy Mason. Backstage Alhambra Theatre Glasgow, 1948. ©Crown Copyright.

Close-season activity at this period usually involved a hectic round of five-a-side competitions.

Thirds were acknowledged masters of this game and, from 13 pre-season events, took top honours, with six winners' medals and four runners-up badges. They played in the following:

Scotstoun Sports.	Winners.
Stranraer Tourney.	Winners.
Edinburgh Sports.	Winners.
Shawfield Sports.	Winners.
Helenvale Sports.	Winners.
6th Bute Tourney.	Winners.

Their rarely-altered "fives" side was:

Balunas, Mason, Orr, Mooney and Staroscik.

An accepted invitation to tour Northern Ireland during the close season also paid dividends in the sense of allowing newcomers to slot in to the Cathkin style and provided a few days of the social benefits of getting to know each other.

The results were as follows:

Linfield	1	Thirds	3
Leinster	2	Thirds	3
Ballymena	1	Thirds	5

They were actually scheduled to leave for a short close-season tour to Poland on 14th May but a late stop was put on this one.

The following XI kicked off the season with Aberdeen in opposition:

Petrie; Balunas, Kelly; Orr, Barclay, Harrower; Staroscik, Mason, Stirling, Ayton, Mitchell.

An Ayton goal in 60 minutes gave Thirds the points.

Early October found Jimmy Ayton requesting a transfer having lost his first-team slot. The pacey, inside man had his request granted but he had to await developments.

Matt Balunas and Johnny Kelly – A superb defensive duo. ©Hi Hi Annual.

November brought a real bombshell with Thirds' long-serving defender Johnny Kelly asking for a move.

The transfer bug became infectious and offers were arriving for Thirds' top trio of Orr, Mitchell and Mason. It was reported that an English club had tabled £45,000 for these stars but this was apparently turned down.

Jimmy Brownlie, a Third Lanark legend of the early 1900s, took part in a real touch of nostalgia prior to a match on Saturday, 2nd April, 1949.

The Thirds match secretary of season 1897 presented former idol Jimmy with a framed photographic history of his Cathkin times.

Over the season, Matt Balunas made most appearances with 39 starts, closely followed by Mason, Harrower and Orr on 36 each.

Scott was leading scorer with 10 and close second came the trio of Mitchell, McCulloch and Staroscik.

Tee Time at Cathkin, 1950 – included in this Group are: Mason, Harrower, Dick, Mooney, Henderson, Balunas, McLeod and Director W. Campbell. ©Associated Newspapers.

League doubles against Celtic and St Mirren cheered the fans, and good home wins over Rangers, Hibernian and Aberdeen were recorded.

The Scottish Cup first round saw Thirds notch an excellent 2-1 win over Aberdeen but they went out to Hearts in the next round.

The cup clash with the Dons left the treasurer happy. A crowd of 22,744 brought in gate monies of £1,546.

It was interesting to note that despite the loss of their left wing duo Mitchell and Mason, who were on league duty against the Irish League, the same day, a Cathkin goal blitz of three in 90 seconds gave Thirds a great 3-2 win against Falkirk, although the Bairns gained revenge in the return game with a crushing 5-1 defeat.

Mason was again missing from the ranks at Brockville as he was performing par excellence for Scotland against Wales, where he scored a

| THE THIRD LANARK ATHLETIC CLUB LTD. | N⁰ 36472 |

THE THIRD LANARK ATHLETIC CLUB LTD.

N⁰ 36472

SCOTTISH CUP FIRST ROUND

T H I R D   L A N A R K
VERSUS
A B E R D E E N

SATURDAY, 22nd JANUARY, 1949
KICK OFF, 2.30 p.m.

TICKET ——— 1/6 ——— (including Tax)

A D M I T   B E A R E R   T O   G R O U N D

Note the price – 7¹/₂p.

goal in their 3-1 victory. These top two Cathkin stars were bringing much acclaim to the club.

The pre-season 1949/50 trial game attracted a crowd of 8,017 fans and they were not disappointed. They watched a new left-wing partnership of former Hibernian stars, Cuthbertson and Baker, perform extremely well and this partially helped them forget the early season departure of favourite Adam McCulloch to Northampton Town.

Both ex-Hibees were included in Thirds' opening side:

Fraser; Balunas, Harvey; Orr, Christie, Mooney; J. Henderson, Mason, Scott, Cuthbertson, Baker.

This season heralded the arrival of another great Cathkin character. The 6th November, 1949 brought the talents of a long-legged, gangly youth to Thirds' left touchline. None other than the redoubtable Ally McLeod!

McLeod played his part in an ordinary match against Stirling Albion which finished 2-4, but the following week Ally enjoyed his first real thrill when he scored against Raith Rovers at Stark's Park.

Peter Russell was appointed trainer on 3rd December following the unexpected resignation of Hugh Good, a stalwart of many years.

In mid-December it was reported that 10 players had put their names to a grievance letter to the board, which prompted a quick reply to the effect that a meeting would be arranged.

This meeting took place within seven days and the players' representative carried back to the complainants assurances on the several matters discussed.

The meeting's outcome must have been satisfactory because, following an horrendous start to the season, Thirds won the next match at Cathkin against Dundee 1-0, with newcomer Dave McKellar in goal.

On 18th February, 1950, another debutant took the field. Lewis Goram's name appeared on the team sheet for the match at Arbroath and although the Red Lichties won 1-0 no blame was attached to Goram for the defeat.

Goram, of course, was the father of the Scotland and Rangers keeper Andy, who has constantly confirmed that his late dad was a real source of inspiration and a superb example of his craft.

Thirds v Dundee at Cathkin. Christie, Bruce (Dundee), "Lewis Goram", Alan Orr.
©Angus Photos Dundee.

Football and Thirds were enjoying a mini boom spell with great attendances. A Scottish-Cup tie with Arbroath attracted 14,323 fans who paid out £840 for the privilege.

In March Jimmy Carabine resigned as manager and this stunned everyone associated with the club. The board announced that there would be no rush to fill the role, and eventually "gentleman" Alec Ritchie was appointed.

In anticipation of the next campaign, Ritchie decided to clear the playing ranks and the following were released:

Baird, Barclay, Croy, Friel, Scott, Jackson, McKellar, Petrie, Thom, Kelly and the amateur Pearson.

Goram decided to move to Bury at the back end of the season and Thirds moved quickly to replace him with a talented teenager in Ronnie Simpson, signed from Queen's Park.

This season brought with it a quite astonishing Scottish Cup second-round tie against Celtic at Cathkin on Saturday, 11th February, 1950. Thirds were ultimately knocked out but no one present will forget the quite amazing scenes at Cathkin that day.

Twenty-five thousand fans had been permitted entry before a blizzard of snow some 30 minutes before kick-off, fell on the park, obliterating the lines and virtually rendering the pitch unplayable.

Following an announcement that the match was postponed, close on 10,000 fans invaded the park. Windows were smashed in the pavilion, a main gate was torn down and players and officials were besieged in the dressing rooms.

Police on duty under an incessant barrage of snowballs, had to radio for foot and mounted reinforcements. Appeals from both Thirds and Celtic officials were drowned in a storm of booing.

Even the ultimate announcement that money would be refunded at Parkhead and Cathkin on the Monday could not pacify the extremists. The cause of all this was genuinely outwith the club's control. Around 2.30pm a very heavy snow storm obliterated the lines and, at 2.55pm, referee George Mitchell of Falkirk had no alternative but to call-off the tie despite attempts to clear the lines on three occasions. Then came the dreaded announcement and possibly the most culpable rider which really had the crowds erupting in fury.

Just on 3.00pm it was announced over the public address system that the teams had agreed to play a friendly. Now without the benefit of knowing then that they would probably still get a refund, the fans generally assumed that they were being taken for a ride, having paid a full entry fee for a "non-event". Extremely bad public relations in retrospect but suffice it to say that bedlam resulted.

The players duly trooped out, lined up and kicked off, before even the Celtic fans saw red. The game was being officiated by Thirds reserve trainer George Clapperton and not George Mitchell. That was the signal for chaos. Not more than three players had touched the ball before thousands of fans poured on to the pitch. Players naturally panicked and made for the pavilion. The crowd chants of "we want our money back" was possibly the forerunner to today's people power, because both clubs immediately agreed to this refund, despite being perfectly aware of the possibility of paying out to non-attenders.

Celtic chairman and Scottish League president Bob Kelly announced the details of refunds to the crowd which did not pacify all. Questions were raised as to how could people get time off work on Monday afternoon to collect a refund and how could Celtic and Thirds possibly know who was at the game?

An attempt was then made to hand out vouchers for redemption but, on several occasions, these were grabbed in bulk and that scheme was buried. Finally, at 4.40pm, the police summoned from every division of the city managed to clear the ground. The final outcome was that the clubs would refund all claimants and Celtic in fact agreed to meet the additional cost of travel in respect of their fans and requested them to submit their claims in writing. The match was re-scheduled for Wednesday but again weather intervened. Celtic eventually moved into round three with a thrilling 4-1 victory .

Neither Thirds nor Celtic were held to blame. However, the Cathkin officials were strongly reminded that in future they must have available at least sufficient numbers of vouchers to hand out in emergencies, to enable the sting to be quickly taken out of this sort of situation.

It was a disappointing season generally. In mid-December Thirds were locked in the basement with only two victories from 13 matches. A late surge, with Goram performing heroics between the sticks, ultimately saved the day and relegation was avoided. They finished second to an excellent Hibernian in the League Cup section.

Of course manager Carabine's resignation, along with that of trainer Good, had affected morale at the club and, when reserve trainer Campbell and groundsman Holmes followed suit, the players were shattered. Carabine's move ended a quite remarkable 20-years association with the club and his presence was sorely missed. Jimmy moved into sports journalism.

Thirds had also been hit financially. Lower attendance figures because of their indifferent results had the treasurer worried. They were badly hit when the SFL decided to cancel the October league game against Rangers, because the Ibrox club had three players in the Scotland pool for the game against Ireland. When the match was finally played on Monday, 1st May, all league issues had been decided and the attendance was dramatically reduced.

Partick Thistle completed a high-scoring double over Thirds in the league. Victories of 5-1 at Firhill and 7-2 at Cathkin were humiliating. At Cathkin the Jags appeared resplendent in a new strip: dark blue jerseys with white sleeves. Perhaps it gave Thistle a European look but it gave Thirds the jitters and a trouncing.

Balunas, Mooney and Dick proved to be Cathkin's most consistent players. Cuthbertson, with 23 goals, took the scoring honours. The ever-presents were Balunas, Jimmy Harrower and Henderson.

A lack of confidence in the Thirds board was being expressed even before a ball was kicked in earnest 1950/51.

There were alleged claims over share irregularities when it was reported that a small shareholder, following his application for shares, had been advised that the Shares Register was closed.

It transpired that, only a few weeks later, blocks of 1,500 and 2,000 shares had been released to a well-known Glasgow businessman!

Explanations were demanded and the reported outcome of a hurriedly-convened board meeting, was that chairman Milne had resigned his position whilst remaining on the board, with the chairmanship going to Mr WH Cowan. John Lawson, became vice-chairman and that was the situation when Thirds commenced the season.

Manager Ritchie was not long in situ, but the fans were already looking for a miracle.

An excellent Ritchie signing did take place pre-season when, on 30th June, he obtained the signature of Ronnie Simpson. This had an unusual twist in completion. Simpson was doing his Army National Service at Catterick Camp. There on that afternoon he sat, Thirds contract in one hand and pen poised in the other. A quick phone call to his Dad, former Ibrox legend Jimmy, was enough for the youngster to accept the terms and sign on the line. What a wonderful future materialised for Simpson, who saw further great fame with Newcastle United, Hibernian and Celtic in a glittering career.

Manager Ritchie expressed great delight also when he managed to secure the services of the one and only Jimmy Mason for a further season on 14th June and the fans certainly were thrilled to be told of this slick piece of work.

Kenny Dawson retired from the active side of the game. His career had brought him thousands of fans who had seen him, over the years, crack in some 209 goals, most with his dynamic left foot. His short Cathkin exploits will never be forgotten.

A rather severe restriction was placed on manager Ritchie as a consequence of the club finishing the previous season in debt. They had lost close to

£2,110 it was recorded and this meant that new signings would be strictly limited.

Better news and prospects, however, were seen at the pre-season trial match on 5th August which pushed one youngster into the limelight. Wattie Dick, playing in the old inside-forward role thrilled the crowd with a superb 90 minutes and four glorious goals.

On Saturday, 12th August, Thirds opened up with the following XI against Raith Rovers at Kirkcaldy:

Simpson; Balunas, Harrower; Orr, Christie, Mooney; Henderson, Mason, Cuthbertson, Dick, Staroscik. Raith won a close fought game 3-2.

An early exit from the Glasgow Cup was followed by an exciting 90 minutes against Rangers at Ibrox, in the semi-final of the Charity Cup.

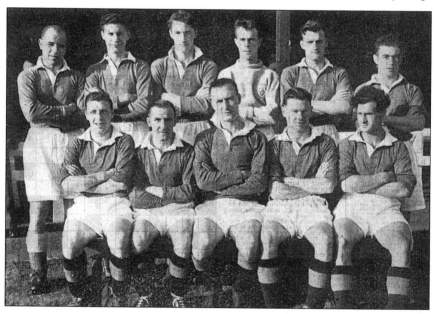

Thirds 1950/51. ©Sporting Mirror.
Balunas, Orr, Christie, Simpson, Harrower, Mooney, Henderson, Mason, Cuthbertson, Dick, Staroscik.

Some 36,700 spectators were thrilled to watch a 1-1 draw and the bulk of them were even more delighted when, after extra time, a correct guess at the toss of the coin took Rangers into the final.

This campaign ended on 14th May with Thirds lining up against Reading in the Festival of Britain Cup, but the Southern outfit emerged victorious by 2-1.

A recorded trading loss of £9,000 for the season showed the reaction of fans to the continuing saga of apparent indifference emanating from "upstairs", which was being reflected on the field of play. Time now surely for new policies and pride.

During the season Thirds had signed George Aitken, Jimmy Bradley, Jimmy Archibald, Jim Duncan, Jim Smellie and Ken Currie.

Leaving Cathkin at this time were Alan Orr, to Nottingham Forest and Feliks Staroscik, to Northampton Town.

A great Scottish Cup run in 1951/52 took Thirds to the semi-finals where Dundee, with a 2-0 scoreline, finished their interest.

An all-round improvement had meant better league results and a thrilling Charity Cup final draw against Clyde enabled Thirds to share the trophy.

The Glasgow Cup remained out of touch.

Newcomers to this campaign included:

Jocky Robertson, Armadale Thistle; Sam Phillips, Annbank United; Bobby Kennedy, Rob Roy; David Simpson, Hibernian; and George Dobbie, Stoneyburn Juniors.

The most prominent departures were Ronnie Simpson, off to Newcastle United and George Aitken, who joined Sunderland.

These moves brought a violent reaction from the fans and this was followed by questions being asked publicly about the whole viability of these departures.

Why does a club like Third Lanark transfer a player of the calibre of Aitken? Only the previous February, statements from the board included a reference to the Aitken signing ... "Aitken will be the mainstay around whom we will build the new Thirds", was one board statement. The "mainstay" lasted six short months. Manager Ritchie faced the questions and explained that this shock departure was due entirely to a need for cash as a consequence of poorer-than-usual attendances. Thirds had, it was reported, taken in around £64,000 in transfer fees over the previous three years and only an estimated £24,000 was paid out for Aitken, Cuthbertson and Simpson. Even with the previous season's reported loss of £9,000 the fans were both angry and puzzled.

George Aitken. ©Evening Citizen.

On the playing field, this was the side which was most representative of the early season:

48

Petrie; Balunas, Harrower; Mooney, Samuel, Aitken; Henderson, Mason, Cuthbertson, Dick, McCall.

The Scottish Cup trail provided the season's highlights. First round games against Celtic, sparked the fuse. Thirds, following a Cathkin draw, beat the Celts at Parkhead and moved in against Hamilton at Douglas Park. Two games were again needed to separate the teams, with Thirds emerging victorious in the replay. The third round paired Thirds and Albion Rovers at Cliftonhill and a win there enabled the Warriors to line up against Falkirk in the quarter-finals at Cathkin on 8th March.

This side took the club into the semi-final: Robertson; Balunas, Cairns; Mooney, Forsyth, Harrower; Henderson, Docherty, Cuthbertson, Mason, McLeod.

A flash of scoring genius from Henderson ensured Thirds beat the Bairns before an excellent crowd of 28,487.

On their day Dundee were reckoned to be the finest team in the country, so Thirds were well prepared for a tough encounter.

The Easter Road semi-finalists lined up - Thirds: Robertson; Balunas, Cairns; Mooney, Forsyth, Harrower; Henderson, Dick, Docherty, Mason, McLeod.

Dundee: Henderson; Follon, Cowan; Gallagher, Cowie, Boyd; Burrell, Patillo, Flavell, Steel, Christie.

Goals from Burrell and Steel sealed Thirds' fate. Steel was reported as having a magnificent match and gave the Cathkin defence a real roasting.

The term had ended, for a pleasant change, in some style and the final quarter's results gave the success-starved fans more than a little hope of improvement.

Matt Balunas carved out his own historical niche when injury midway through the first half of the season forced him to miss only his second game in a consecutive four-year spell.

On 8th December, Thirds welcomed a new goalkeeper to the ranks, who was to become one of the finest club servants ever. Jocky Robertson arrived from Armadale Thistle and made a most impressive debut at Broomfield.

September had brought Jimmy Docherty from Doncaster and, some weeks later, another giant, in every sense, donned the Thirds colours when Adam Forsyth moved across the city from Firhill. This was an inspired signing and Adam went on to become a real Cathkin hero.

Never a dull moment on the signing front at this time. George Dobbie,a striker who had an instinctive eye for a half-chance, was signed and, despite regular appearances being restricted by his National Service duties, George also gave great service to the club.

On his debut against Stirling Albion, Dobbie grabbed a delightful double.

An improvement in the club's finances was revealed, when a profit of £8,700 was declared at the AGM.

Adam Forsyth. ©Hi Hi Annual.

At the meeting there was a question raised concerning the comparison of stand season tickets costs with those for Ibrox.

It appeared that both Thirds and Rangers stand "seasons" were priced similarly and this despite the obvious variance in performance and comforts. The Cathkin board stood firm and replied: "You are nearer the action at Cathkin." The cost remained £4!

In season 1952/53, Thirds did not live up to expectations and were relegated. They managed only eight victories in the league.

Line up at Start of Season, 1952/53. ©P A Smith Glasgow.
Phillips, Gordon, Petrie, Kennedy, Duncan, Jamieson, Goodall, Miller, Dobbie, McGuffie,
McLeod.

Of course they had lost the services of some stalwarts along the way. Jimmy Mason had been forced to retire prematurely. Manager Ritchie had fallen prey to a long bout of ill health and the outcome was a sad lack of consistency or enthusiasm on the field of play.

Mason's absence followed an almost uninterrupted 16-plus Cathkin years. Fans reluctantly had to accept that he was virtually irreplaceable. More astonishing it was to find that the "maestro" was not called upon in an official capacity with any club to pass on his quite unique talents. Jimmy Mason was tragically allowed to disappear from the game. Other than in a brief coaching role at Dumbarton, Scottish football chose to allow the genius of the man to slide into obscurity.

The Scottish Cup run again proved enthralling. A narrow win at Elgin was followed by a comfortable victory in the borders, which set Thirds up for a tilt against Hamilton. Having disposed of the Lanarkshire lads, they moved on to play Clyde at Shawfield, where, against all the odds, they booked a semi-final spot, with Aberdeen being their opponents.

Incidentally, Jackie Liddell became instant hero at Shawfield with both goals against the Bully Wee.

Thirds definitely had their chances in the first semi-final but a combination of some bad luck and poor finishing let the Dons off the hook.

Aberdeen made sure in the replay. The teams were:

Thirds: Robertson; Balunas, Harrower; Mooney, Forsyth, Duncan; Dobbie, Henderson, Cuthbertson, Dick Bradley.

Aberdeen: Martin; Mitchell, Shaw; Harris, Young, Allister; Rodger, Yorston, Buckley, Hay, Hather.

In local competitions, Thirds fell to Partick Thistle and Celtic, although losing out in the Charity Cup only to the toss of the coin against the Bhoys.

Back in August, the following XI comprised the opening side:

Robertson; Balunas, Cairns; Mooney, Forsyth, Harrower; Goodall, Mason, Heron, Dick, McLeod.

Gil Heron was signed from Celtic just prior to kick off and of course became Thirds' first Jamaican player. He scored twice on his debut.

It was reported then that Thirds had lost close on £3,245 in the previous season. Despite a good cup run with Celtic, the general attendances had been in keeping with results — disastrous!

Manager Ritchie brought great joy to the fans when he announced the following re-signings for the next season:

Robertson, Forsyth, Phillips, Dick and Duncan.

The clear objective was a prompt return to the top, but could it be done?

The club suffered a tragic loss during season 1953/54 with the death of manager Alex Ritchie, following a lengthy illness. This quiet man had given a lot for the Cathkin cause but poor health finally took its full toll.

The handsome Glasgow Charity Cup found its resting place at Cathkin, although they just failed to get promotion, finishing a gallant third to Kilmarnock and Motherwell. A quarter-final spot in the League Cup, only to be defeated by Hibernian, was most encouraging. Rangers took the Glasgow Cup in a stirring final against Thirds, to obtain some revenge for the Hi Hi grabbing the Charity from their grasp.

Thirds won the Ibrox five-a-side tournament against the hosts to give their fans a nice pre-season starter and their hopes were justified in the opening match when they lined up to face Alloa Athletic with St Johnstone and Cowdenbeath completing their League Cup section. They hit an amazing 10 goals into the Alloa net in the opener.

A representative side of the early season would be along the following lines:

Robertson; Phillips, Harrower; Docherty, Forsyth, Muir; Brolls, Maule, Dobbie, Dick, McLeod.

The Scottish Cup may have brought a touch of romance but really not much more. Thirds were paired with Stenhousemuir and it took them three games to dispose of the Larbert side. Deveronvale from the Highland League were the next visitors to Cathkin and they shocked their hosts by taking an early lead. Thirds literally camped in the 'Vale half throughout but yet again a combination of careless finishing and some superb goalkeeping by the visiting keeper, kept the home scoreline blank. Then the bubble finally burst and, in the closing spell, a barrage of goals in 21 minutes brought back the colour to Cathkin cheeks and helped Thirds finally triumph 7-2.

They were then drawn against Rangers, and it took the Light Blues three games to end Thirds' hopes of cup glory. Even in the final game there was a great measure of controversy about Rangers' third goal, which gave them victory.

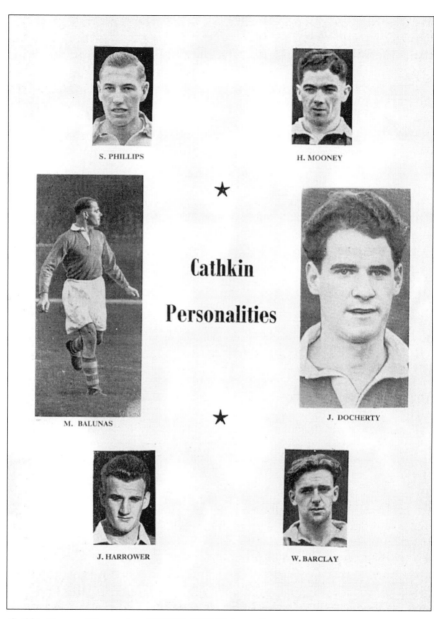

Cathkin Personalities – circa 1953/54. ©Hi Hi Annual.

They called it speculation at board level, with a view to accumulating a big gate when Thirds played Queen of the South reserves on the morning of a Hampden Park International match between Scotland and England. It was reckoned that those going early to the big game would perhaps stop off at Cathkin for an early-morning appetiser. No such luck, the gate monies being £5.2/6!

A most interesting name appeared as Thirds main striker for the Glasgow Cup final against Rangers on 28th September, 1953.

Some perhaps may remember that former Queen of the South centre-forward Billy Houliston played a few games at Cathkin at this time.

Thirds team: Robertson; Balunas, Phillips; Docherty, Forsyth, Duncan; Brolls, Henderson, Houliston, Dick, McLeod.

Billy completed five games for Thirds but, in the one against Rangers,even he could not find the net as Thirds went down 3-0.

Cuthbertson was transferred to Stenhousemuir late in the season and Mooney, that Cathkin dynamo, also asked away. He was encouraged to stay, however, and did for another 18 months.

The highlight came in the season's final match, which saw Thirds, against all odds, defeat Rangers 1-0 to take home the Charity Cup.

Cathkin was under the new chairmanship of WW Campbell, a real Cathkin stalwart in season 1954/55 and, in his opening comments in the handbook, he pointed out the fact that it becomes increasingly difficult to obtain promotion on two specific counts. New players take time to adjust and, of course, each year the second division clubs improve in quality.

Jimmy Blair came in as manager and this former player's pedigree gave every confidence of his ability to take Thirds along the desired course to promotion.

The following new players were brought in Thomson, McCrae, Jamieson, Hardie, Rae, Workman, Gallagher.

Players going out from Cathkin included Balunas, Harrower and Dick, and their combined experience would be sorely missed.

Once again pre-season activity included the "fives" and Thirds won both the Lanarkshire and Rangers Sports.

At Shawfield the score was: Thirds 2 Clyde 1, with Barclay scoring both goals.

At Ibrox, Thirds beat Partick Thistle 2-1. A singularly rare feat occurred at the Ibrox meeting with Ally McLeod scoring all Thirds' six goals in the tournament.

When the fans started flocking back this season, they were delighted to find that a new covered enclosure accommodating 12,000 had been erected. The cost was reported to be £8,000. Director Cowan reminded fans that the club's objective was to provide seated accommodation for everyone - 38 years prior to the Taylor report!

Inside man Jimmy Docherty demanded a transfer following a dispute with the club after his refusal to include himself in the team picture, along with the others who had won the Charity Cup earlier that year. Bobby Kennedy had not arrived for the photo call and Docherty who had played in the previous two rounds but not the final was asked to stand in. Despite having a reasonable claim to be included, having scored the goal that took Thirds into the final itself, he absolutely refused. He was immediately put on the transfer list and had his wages revised to £3 with a £4 bonus for winning. The original agreement was for the basic £7 plus £4 bonus.

The Cathkin board in July 1954 announced that ALL players, both signed or unsigned, would be available for transfer and this just two weeks before the start of the season.

Five stalwarts had still to put pen to paper. They were Robertson, Balunas, Harrower, Docherty and Dick.

Just seven days later these "rebels" re-signed and all was forgotten as the board invited the Charity Cup-winning squad to a golf outing at Strone, followed by dinner at which the winners' medals were presented. Well, this was Third Lanark!

In December, 1954, Jack Marshall intimated that, due to ill-health, he would be resigning from the board, with immediate effect. It was simultaneously confirmed that his replacement would be a Glasgow businessman of comparative youthful years, who had a tremendous affection for Thirds. That statement signalled the first appearance centre stage of Bill Hiddleston at Cathkin Park, in an official capacity.

At this time the unavoidable outcome of Harrower's persistent transfer requests was his eventual move to Accrington Stanley in December, 1954, for a reported £2,000. Two years previously, Manchester City were prepared to part with £12,000 for Jimmy. Now, two years on and his displays confirming his abilities being as good as ever, his value was only £2,000. On this basis it is certain that an 'O' Level in arithmetic was not in the possession of the Cathkin negotiators.

Midway through the season Thirds went on a nine-goal spree against Ayr. Dick got four, Brolls and Miller two each plus a single from Barclay. Bickerstaffe stood in stoically for Robertson during the season when the wee man was off injured but Jocky's sheer presence was sadly missed.

Friendlies at the back end of the season saw Thirds lose out to Accrington, 1-0, whilst at Watford they went down 2-1.

In the Scottish Cup they defeated Queen of the South 2-1 at Cathkin, but went out to Motherwell by 3-1.

Early exits were experienced in both Glasgow and Charity Cups. Rangers, on both occasions, were too good for the Hi Hi.

Season 1955/56 was not long in progress when the services of manager Blair and trainer Bobby Reid were dispensed with purely on the grounds of economy. They severed links with the club on 5th November 1955. It was reported that Thirds' weekly budget was a minimum of £250 and these joint departures could save around £2,000 per annum.

To support this contentious claim, the board reminded all fans that only once during the season had they been able to hand over more cash than the agreed guaranteed sum of £150 to visitors and that happened with Queen's Park's visit to Cathkin when the gate monies amounted to £314.

Ally McLeod was sold to St Mirren and the reason for his transfer was reported to be the urgent need for cash. McLeod's fee was stated at £8,000. At this time Mr Hiddleston was appointed director/manager of the club and this gave the press a field day. Reports of the appointment carried supporting comments to suggest that he had been a Hi Hi fan since he was six years old and was full of unbounded enthusiasm for the club.

Cathkin's new "action man" was early quoted as saying: "I will take Thirds to success."

Manager Hiddleston's first game in charge resulted in a 6-1 hammering from Morton which was immediately followed by cries from fans and shareholders of "crisis".

Another defeat from Forfar Athletic, 3-1, added to the discontent.

Hiddleston was then reported as having made approaches to Ibrox for the loan services of John Prentice and Willie Paton but to no avail.

Of course, his enterprise was quickly taken up by the media and press support for his drive was great. "With such unswerving enthusiasm and determination at the helm the old Thirds must take on a new look," was one of several quotes.

But the disastrous series of results continued with Thirds taking a 5-1 defeat from Cowdenbeath at Cathkin. Thirds' side that day included no fewer than five signings made the previous week. Workman, Archibald, Craig, Gray and Duchart.

They finally recorded their first win in eight outings when they beat Dumbarton 1-0. In goal for Thirds was the one and only Jimmy Cowan, having signed after a 14-month absence through injury.

Economy and Third Lanark were synonomous but it was still incredible to read of one event at Cathkin in one of Scotland's leading sports papers.

This item stated that the two Bills - Hiddleston and Campbell -had spent the previous Sunday at the ground, cleaning and polishing the players' footwear!

Found in the same sports pages was details of Thirds' latest signing. Motherwell's Willie Redpath had joined up and made his debut against Arbroath at Gayfield, on 17th December, 1955, when Thirds lost 1-0.

Yet another playing revival later in the season helped the club gain 30 league points and respectability.

The Sunday Mail sports pages on 18th March, 1956 carried an article headed "Cathkin board Upheaval". A quote from Bill Hiddleston read: "My ultimatum to the board is either 'you go or I go'." In early January Hiddleston had been invited to speak to the Thirds' fans at one of their regular meetings in the Dixon Halls. He was told then: "You are a man after our own hearts but what if you're frustrated in the Boardroom." His reply was: "If I'm the victim of obstruction either I go or they go." Things had come to a head following an undisclosed incident after a game at Brechin a few weeks previously, in which Hiddleston was not involved. He spoke his mind freely at a subsequent board meeting and his views carried much weight.

It was then rumoured that board members John Lawson, John Thomson and Willie Cowan would resign. It was further stated that Hiddleston was only persuaded to stay as a result of influential friends bringing their support to bear.

On the playing front, a most notable absentee this season was Jocky Robertson, who had been 28 weeks on the sidelines in addition to 22 weeks at the back end of the previous campaign due to severe fractures of three fingers. His loss was great for the club and Jocky received a warm welcome back to duty against St Johnstone at Perth in April, where, although on the losing side, he reminded fans of what they had missed.

Youngsters Crabtree and Hanson had slotted in well in Jocky's absence but their inexperience was at times evident, not surprisingly.

League results were interesting. The 9-0 demolition job carried out on Montrose kept the fans happy. Brolls and Craig each scored three, with Gray, Duchart and Kennedy completing the rout.

On Saturday, 12th May, 1956, the curtain came down on the season, to leave Thirds fans on cloud nine.

They won the Glasgow Charity Cup with a side boosted by three guests, Bobby Mitchell, Ivor Broadis and Tommy Docherty. A 4-2 win over Partick Thistle was well deserved.

Broadis, Mitchell and Docherty were among those invited to the Glasgow City Chambers for the official presentation of winners' medals. This prompted the big question: Would Thirds attempt to buy these stars and parade them regularly in the colours? Alas, even if they had traded in their new enclosure they would not have had sufficient cash to turn this dream into reality. So, it was on to the next season, with great hope.

Thirds and Clyde were the exceptions to a clean sweep of Glasgow clubs being in the First Division, in season 1956/57. Could they both make it this year?

Hiddleston, when asked, replied: "Of course, although football is no longer a game, it is finance now." This quote, it is worth remembering, was made many years ago and by this accountant, public house owner and at that particular time, concrete layer, who happened to be doing just that on the Cathkin terracings when approached for his views!

The enquirer was then given a personal tour of the stadium with the various anomalies being pointed out. "Sure the stand is rusty, the accommodation is not right, the pavilion would be best swept away but," Hiddleston went on, "look at the potential." "What we really need is a new stand and new terracing. I think we could comfortably hold up to a maximum of 50,000 fans."

He pointed to another area of the ground, behind Cathkin and said: "A well-known builder wants to erect houses there and maybe we'll let him, because we own the ground." How many fans attend regularly?, he was then asked. "Oh, around 7,000, although recently gates have been as low as 1,800. But we are developing a youth policy. For example our assistant manager Bobby Bowman is 35 and we have signed 18 players with an average age of 23 and this includes seniors like Redpath and Roy." That then, was the Hiddleston outlook at that time.

Thirds won promotion thanks to a late winning burst which brought them second top spot to Clyde, to complete the scenario of all the Glasgow clubs, being in the First Division.

Fifty-one points had been gathered and, in the process, an amazing 105 goals were scored. Thirds only lost nine games in total in the league. Interesting to recall the regulars wearing the colours then:

Robertson; Smith, Brown; Kennedy, Lewis, Kelly; McInnes, Craig, Allan, Roy, Walker, Stewart, Wark.

Whilst the league displays were impressive, the cup involvement was disappointing. Dundee United knocked Thirds out of the Scottish Cup 5-2 and they lost out in both the Glasgow and Charity Cups courtesy of Clyde and Partick Thistle respectively.

Mid-season found two directors resigning, Messrs Thomson and Cowan relinquished their posts for personal reasons.

Thirds, it was reported, had shown a profit for the previous season of £3,500, although this sum was subsequently questioned at a board meeting.

Few Cathkinites will ever forget the dramatic debut of left winger Joe McInnes in August, 1956. Signed only four hours prior to kick-off, a devastating display ended with him netting five glorious goals to help Thirds trounce Stenhousemuir 8-2. Joe's personal tally must still be a record for a left-wing debutant. The final season's total of 105 goals was Thirds' second highest ever.

Whilst the strike rate kept the fans thrilled, spare a thought for sides like Stenhousemuir, who conceded nine goals in the League Cup and 10 more in the league to the Cathkin hot-shots.

Other big wins came with the 7-0 drubbing of Dumbarton, with both Forfar and Montrose conceding six. Morton, St Johnstone and East Stirling also found the Thirds forwards too hot to handle and lost five, six and four goals respectively.

All action Johnny Kelly made a real impact on his debut at Boghead and Thirds introduced ex-Firhill star Jimmy Walker to their fans at Tannadice in the Scottish Cup.

The 5-2 scoreline in favour of Dundee United was one Walker was not likely to forget. However, Jimmy brought smiles to the faithful with a hat-trick against East Stirling only two weeks later.

Wearing the number nine jersey at this time was recently-signed Johnny Allan, formerly of Aberdeen, and it took him only three games to bag his first hat-trick against Stenhousemuir at Cathkin.

Certainly the match of the campaign for Thirds fans, was against Alloa at Cathkin on 2nd January, 1957. The visitors romped to a three goal lead in the opening 45 minutes but Thirds were finally stung into retaliation and took both points, thanks to a remarkable last- minute fourth goal from George Dobbie.

Allan – Scoring against Queen's Park keeper Ferguson. ©Scottish Football Book.

Changes galore at least grabbed the fans' interest and the arrival of Herbert from Doncaster Rovers kept the pot boiling. He provided lots of dash and attacking spirit and helped Thirds achieve an excellent 6-1 win on his debut against Forfar Athletic.

The Cathkin boys gained revenge for their early Scottish Cup exit at Tannadice when they returned the following week on league business and won 1-0.

Despite promotion being won, there were still question marks over the harmony within the club. Cries for resignation had been made and Bill Hiddleston offered to resign following further disagreement. The board apparently had taken strong objection to his querying the previous season's profit figure. The outcome of much deliberation came with the resignation of Hiddleston.

In December, Thirds appointed Reuben Bennett from Ayr as trainer. Later he went on to much greater fame with Liverpool.

Despite the recurring, board-room capers, the faithful could not wait for the start of Thirds first appearance with the big boys after five long years.

Season 1957/58 was one of consolidation and predictably difficult, so to finish in 14th place was just about acceptable.

The following pool of players had achieved this:

Robertson, Herd, Stewart, Brown, H Smith, W Smith, Cosker, Lewis, Kelly, Reid, Slingsby, McCrae, McInnes, R Craig, W Craig, Catterson, Carmichael, Cunningham, Allan, Townsend, Harley, Gray.

Easily identified in this list will be three-fifths of the future "ton-up brigade", McInnes, Harley and Gray.

Other stars to appear on the Cathkin horizon during this campaign were Ramage and Ian Hilley.

The board made one of their best-ever signings, when Bob Shankly agreed to become manager on a full-time basis.

His arrival coincided with the entry fee to games being increased to 2/6 and he was promised that the additional 6d per fan, (2.5pence) would be his for new signing business required!!

Thirds finished well clear of the danger zone and scored 69 goals in the process, although their defence certainly required tightening, having lost 88 goals.

Ex-Don, Johnny Allan, took third top place in the Scottish League personal scoring stakes with an excellent 36 league goals (39 in all competitions).

With Shankly quite determined to raise standards all round, the normally questionable plea for patience from the board was acknowledged on this occasion as being reasonable.

Newly promoted side of 1958. ©Scottish Football Book.
Smith, Brown, Robertson, Kelly, Lewis, Slingsby, W. Craig, R. Craig, Allan, Cunningham, McInnes.

Season 1958/59 was highlighted by a Scottish Cup semi-final appearance.

The spectre of Second Division again reared its ugly head when Thirds went through November and December with only one win.

Come the turn of the year and a terrific run of results, with 13 wins from 15 matches, enabled them to reach safety and, in the process, give the fans real value for money.

Hearts became the Hi Hi bogey men. Thirds lost 12 league goals and eight League Cup counters to the Edinburgh side.

Dick registered a hat-trick against Queen of the South, whilst Matt Gray got two trebles, in games with Raith Rovers and Motherwell.

Thirds struck with a vengeance in tilts with Queen of the South and Dunfermline. They put 12 goals into the Dumfries net and 10 past the Pars' keeper.

The first team squad was: Robertson; Kelly, McCallum; Robb, Ramage, Lewis; Caldwell, Brown, D Hilley, R Craig, W Dick, M Gray, McInnes, Goodfellow, Harley.

A fitness fanatic, Tom McNiven arrived to take charge of training and this appointment superbly complemented the Shankly managerial style.

An excellent Scottish Cup run ended at the semi-final stage when Thirds came second best to Aberdeen in a replay.

Clyde knocked the Hi Hi out of the Charity Cup and they lost out narrowly in the Glasgow Cup when, after beating Celtic in round one Rangers took the honours in the semi-final by 2-1.

No stopping the fans raised hopes for the coming season, however, with more than enough talent available under the guidance of Shankly to bring success.

Would Thirds at last travel first-class in season 1959/60 and lose the Cinderella tag amongst the Glasgow clubs?

Jimmy Goodfellow. An integral part of the High Scoring front line of Season 1960/61. ©Scottish Football Book.

New floodlights were installed at Cathkin in October but what about the playing prospects under this much brighter scrutiny?

Kelly had departed and Jimmy Robb's National Service duties restricted his appearances, but the Cathkin pool looked strong:

Robertson, Ramage, Caldwell, Smith, Brown, Cunningham, Harvey, McCormack, Robb, Slingsby, H Smith, Cosker, Lewis, McCallum, D Hilley, I Hilley, R Craig, Goodfellow, Welsh, Dick, Gray, Harley, McIntyre, McInnes, Gow.

The much sought-after ingredients of "harmony and unity" had arrived this season. Their timely appearance was credited to the formation of a new board, in addition to the Shankly/McNiven combine.

Board members listed at the beginning of the campaign were:

Chairman, FT Martin; vice-chairman, W McLean; directors, George Foster, R Spence, James Murray (Secretary); honorary treasurer, C Dow.

The fans really appreciated Shankly's pre-season comment: "I will only sign players who want to play for Thirds.".... Perhaps not an original thought, but a highly-motivated premise.

Two last-minute pre-season signings were testament to Shankly's expertise on "quality". Jim Reilly and Junior McGillivray arrived and what a superb double capture this was.

In their League Cup section, Thirds were along with Clyde, Dunfermline and St Mirren.

A formidable task but one which the club tackled with gusto. They stormed into the quarter-final stages, dropping only one point to Clyde at Shawfield.

Their quarter-final tie against Falkirk, whom they beat narrowly at Cathkin 2-1, was followed by the return match at Brockville. On this occasion Thirds triumphed with a fine 3-1 victory.

The semi-final match against Arbroath at Ibrox was comfortably won 3-0 and the scene was set for the final against Hearts on Saturday, 24th October, 1959. This match report appears later.

The spectre of relegation loomed from late October into January. In this period only three points from a possible 26 had been gathered. The great escape materialised, however, with 15 points taken from the next 13 matches in a storming run-in.

The season ended on a high with a fine 2-1 victory against Rangers at Ibrox.

It must be accepted that much of the reason for this closeness to the drop was caused by injuries to key players. At one time or another, McCallum, Lewis, Hilley and McInnes had been absent for some weeks.

Star youngster George McCallum was sadly forced to take early retirement from football in his mid 20s, due to a series of nasty injuries. It was a sad loss to Thirds and football in general.

Ever present skipper Jim Reilly proved to be the club's best buy that season with a series of unrivalled displays.

A mid-table league placing along with the League Cup runners-up spot brought great credit to Thirds and made it a season to remember.

Despite Jocky Robertson performing heroics in goal against Clyde in the Scottish Cup at Shawfield, the Bully Wee won the day with two late strikes. Clyde also ended Thirds' interest in the Glasgow Cup, with Partick Thistle doing likewise in the Charity Cup.

George Young succeeded Shankly as manager following the League Cup final and worked diligently to steer them clear of relegation.

Amongst his priorities for further success for the club was the need to go full-time. But would he be able to convince the board of the viability of such a costly step?

Because of the quite tremendous separate influence the events of seasons 1960/61, 1964/65 and 1966/67 eventually had on the club's ultimate demise, they are examined collectively, later in the book.

Let's, however, move on to season 1961/62. Never before had Thirds' Jekyll & Hyde tendencies been so cruelly exposed. They slumped to 11th place in the league, due almost entirely to the forwards being completely off the goal standard.

The season kicked off with problems galore, not the least being the Hilley, Harley and Gray "better terms or transfer" demands.

Their unrest continued virtually throughout the season. Failure to qualify for a League Cup quarter-final spot, was followed by a Scottish Cup defeat by Celtic after a replay.

Thirds failed to collect a single point against Dundee, Rangers, Aberdeen and Falkirk. It could be argued that the Bairns' two league wins against Thirds saved the Brockville Boys from relegation.

Matt Gray in action. Prolific scorer – 98 Goals in 167 Matches.
©Daily Record.

Thirds had an amazing 7-2 victory over Dundee United at Cathkin but lost the return game 3-0.

Alex Harley remained top marksman with 33 goals, including a four, a three and two penalty conversions. Matt Gray came second in the scoring stakes with 29.

Twenty players were used in the campaign with Gray, the only ever present. Bill Clarkston made his debut at centre-half in the final league game.

An announcement was made to advise that the coming close season would witness the demolition of the grand stand to be replaced with a modern version.

Thirds sojourn in Europe was brief. In the Franco/British Cup they lost both home and away to Rouen, from France, by 2-1.

On paper the following pool had looked extremely useful but in the event a combination of re-signing problems and injuries to top players produced only mediocrity.

The squad: Robertson, McGillivray, Cunningham, McCormack, McLeod, McKinlay, McCallum, Lewis, Gray, McCool, McInally, McInnes, Hilley, Harley, Reilly, Goodfellow.

Manager George Young and trainer Tom McNiven completed the management team.

Board resignations, managerial changes and player unrest ensured another season of discontent in 1962/63.

The outcome was that Thirds managed to avoid the drop by only three points.

Manager Young, along with three directors walked out on the club in mid-December, following the return of Mr Hiddleston to the board. George Foster became chairman and Airdrie boss Willie Steel accepted the offer to replace Young as manager at Cathkin.

Messrs Spence, Meadows and McMillan completed the board.

Thirds were plunged into a powerful League Cup section with Rangers, Hibernian and St Mirren. Not a single point was taken from these clubs and it was not until 10th November that Thirds grabbed a win, when they beat Airdrie at Broomfield 4-1.

The previous nine matches had brought five points, from as many draws.

Two weeks after the Broomfield game, Thirds beat Dundee 4-2 to again take the points.

Of course, any club which had lost the services of players like Harley, Hilley and Gray, could not expect to be on a winning streak.

They used 26 players in this season, with McGillivray the only perfect attender.

Thirds drew East Fife in the Scottish Cup and it took them three matches to better the Fifers. Raith Rovers, in the next round, avenged their Fife neighbours when they defeated Thirds at Cathkin 1-0.

For the first time since 1909, the Glasgow Cup was won by Thirds when they beat Celtic 2-1 at Hampden.

The winning team was:

Robertson; McGillivray, Davis; Reilly, Lewis, Baird; Goodfellow, Spence, Cunningham, McMorran, McInnes.

Former Thirds favourite Bobby Craig played for the Celts but even his spells of magic could not prevent a success for the Warriors.

Sammy Baird, incidentally, captained Thirds and it is ironic that this short-term signing collected a winner's medal when so many long-serving Cathkin players had left the club empty-handed.

At this stage the team lists were regularly peppered with "Newman Trialist, and AN Other" such was the vagaries of player selection and availability.

The Glasgow Cup win was almost the solitary high in a season of lows.

It was apparent that unless a period of stability was again established at board level there was not much hope for real progress.

Cynics were asking: "Surely the time had not arrived when a match programme purchase was required to identify board members - or had it?"

It is a sad reflection to find that Matt Gray, despite leaving Thirds midway through the season, finished top scorer with 13 goals.

The registered player pool for season 1963/64 was:

Paul, Mitchell, Lewis, McGillivray, Davis, Locke, McCormack, Cunningham, Little, McKay, Hewitt, Brownlie, Geddes, Dickson, Murray, Todd, Kerr, Paterson, Graham, Black, Anderson, Buckley, McLeod, McMorran, Bryce.

A clear-out of players saw 19 being released during the close season. Newcomers included a mixture of veterans and youth.

Goalkeeper Stuart Mitchell arrived from Newcastle United, Ken Brownlie from Pittodrie and Max Murray from Ibrox, as well as returned exile Ally McLeod from Hibernian.

Jim McMorran, a classy inside man, completed the newcomers and the following "team of strangers" took the field against Dundee in the opening League Cup encounter:

Mitchell; McGillivray, Davis; Brownlie, McCormack, Cunningham; Todd, Anderson, Murray, McMorran and McLeod.

Dundee won 2-1 and, from the above team list, it will be seen that Thirds had lost, among others, the entire "100-up" strike force of the early 60s.

In retrospect Mr Hiddleston had this to say about the season under review: "We have too many worries about relegation and, even when we escaped the axe, there appeared further danger in the attempts of other clubs to chop five sides from the first division." Even in the mid-60s, league reconstruction was much in the mind. Hiddleston added: "It has been said that football at Cathkin will cease as the ground is to be sold for building purposes and so on. I assure you all that this is absolute nonsense."

These actual comments can be found in the club handbook of 1964/65.

Mid-season brought another two new men to Cathkin. Mike Jackson crossed over from Parkhead and young Pat Buckley joined up from Preston Athletic. Jackson, particularly, had good cause to remember his arrival day, as he ultimately had to buy his own transfer on departure.

Following a dismal run of defeats, Thirds beat St. Mirren at Cathkin on 22nd February 4-2. Jim McMorran that day became the local hero with a scintillating display of good old-fashioned inside-forward work. He scored all four goals to make it his day to remember.

Assurances were given by the board, as the season drew to a close but, for the fans, it was very much a "wait-and-see" situation, with great trepidation about the prospects come August.

We move on to season 1965/66 when Thirds finished in the bottom half of the league and in this, their penultimate campaign, the spectre of uncertainty was a constant companion to the on-field efforts.

The opening 11 against Hamilton was:

Williams; Connell, Baillie; Jackson, Little, McKay; Miller, McLaughlin, Fyfe, J Kilgannon, and Henderson.

Later in the season, the above side, with May replacing Jackson, almost pulled off a shock result against Hibernian in the Scottish Cup.

In April 1966, former war-time guest Frank Joyner accepted the managerial role and quickly enlisted the help of Bobby McCallum as trainer.

These two had a quite prodigious appetite for work and their diligence and enthusiasm for a Cathkin revival was never in doubt. Circumstances completely outwith their control defused this vital spark and virtually ended any outside chance of success.

The most damning indictment levelled at Thirds came in the form of a press item which highlighted the fact that over a few short years the club had released or transferred a team of stars:

Evan Williams, Finlay McGillivray, Joe Davis, Jim Reilly, John McCormack, Willie Cunningham, Dave Hilley, Alex. Harley, Matt Gray, Pat Buckley, Jocky Robertson, Joe McInnes, Jim McMorran, Jim Goodfellow.

Frequent promises were given by the board with regard to the club's future but these utterances just could not prevent the faithful from believing that all signs remained extremely ominous and that Thirds were drawing dangerously close to an end.

Club scouts had been hovering ready to swoop on any likely Cathkin player put on the transfer list. The first move came in February 1966, when Wolves enticed Evan Williams to Molyneux Park, with Robert Russell from Stenhousemuir being signed as it transpired as a most capable replacement.

Third Lanark had now moved from the back pages to the front of most national newspapers. The club was certainly in dreadful turmoil.

Questions were being asked publicly:

"Would Thirds be around in August?"
"Would they be playing at Cathkin?"
"Would Bishopbriggs, or East Kilbride be their new home?"

Even then no one could have foretold the quite horrendous catalogue of events which was still to overtake this club during their final season. However, many fans were conspicuous by their absence come August 1966.

It is prudent now to examine closely the three specific seasons involved in the ultimate downfall and look in some depth at the trials and tribulations which brought about the end ...

CHAPTER 3

THE ULTIMATE DOWNFALL

In July 1960, under the chairmanship of W McLean, a most ambitious board took the financial plunge and Thirds went full-time.

The final league game of season 1960-61 more than repaid the confidence generated by this move, when Hi Hi climaxed a thrilling year and gave their success-starved fans a day and season to remember.

The following team lined up on Saturday 29th April, 1961, against Hibernian.

Robertson, McGillivray, Lewis; Reilly, McCormack, Cunningham; Goodfellow, Hilley, Harley, Gray, McInnes.

The Fans Dream XI. ©Scottish Football Book.
Back row: Reilly, McCormack, McGillivray, Robertson, Cunningham, Lewis.
Front row: Goodfellow, Hilley, Harley, Gray, McInnes.

With only eight minutes remaining and the scoreline 5-1 in Thirds' favour, Cathkin exploded into a cauldron of hate with the man at the centre being none other than former Cathkin keeper Ronnie Simpson.

Dave Hilley had left a string of defenders in his wake as he burst into the Hibs penalty box and, with only Simpson to beat for that glorious 100th league goal of the season, he was impeded and barged to the ground. No question a penalty! It took a couple of minutes to revive Hilley before Thirds scoring star Alex Harley stepped forward to beat Simpson from the spot. Red scarves were thrown on to the park and hundreds of youngsters invaded the pitch where hero Harley was mobbed by team-mates and fans alike.

The emotional atmosphere surrounded what was really Thirds' own cup final and the prevailing spirit had never been more pronounced. The desire for success had been so great that at one point during that memorable match the referee actually had to separate two Thirds players Gray and Harley for discussing rather heatedly an earlier Gray "miss". Needless to say, all was forgotten and forgiven on the final whistle!

"Harley makes it 100". ©Hi Hi Annual.

The odds against the Hi Hi achieving the 100 goals before this game were around 14-1. Thirds were two up in three minutes with Gray and Hilley scoring. Then Harley made it three just before the break. Two Harley penalties including the "century" conversion and a slick Reilly goal in the second-half gave Thirds the most historic six goals in their history.

A quite remarkable performance and Harley's hat-trick made him Scotland's leading scorer for the season with a superb total of 42 goals.

Thirds lost 80 goals yet that was really immaterial because the magic 100 scored meant sufficient points had been won to attain an outstanding third top league place.

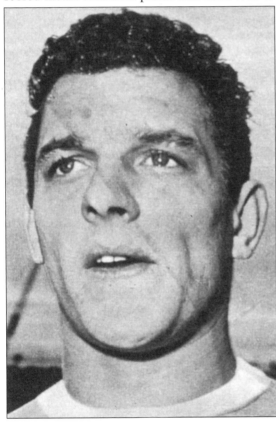

Thirds league position, their 100 goals and the Harley individual scoring feat answered 'any' critics of full-time football.

Twelve players initially accepted the new full-time deal and had enjoyed a new Cathkin Training Plan.

Five-days-a-week training, morning and afternoon, included lunch at the club at a subsidised cost to players of only 2/- (10p) per day.

The reasoning behind manager George Young's full-time scheme was extremely sound. George explained as follows:

Ace Marksman Alex Harley. ©Hi Hi Annual.

A. HARLEY

J. GOODFELLOW

D. HILLEY

M. GRAY

J. McINNES (*Sunday Post*)

Thirds Hot Shots. ©Hi Hi Annual.
Harley, Gray, Hilley, Goodfellow, McInnes.

Fun & Frolics at Cathkin & West Kilbride Beach, 1961. Groups include: Manager George Young and Players Reilly, McLeod, Gray, Hilley, Harley, McInnes, McGillivray and McCormack. ©Daily Record.

"Last season we lost 10 games out of 14 by the odd goal and, in eight of these, we were actually leading. Our new training methods will ensure that the players are toughened up to last the full 90 minutes and resist these late challenges which have been so costly."

The League Cup-ties gave Thirds a chance to test their sharpness from day one. Home and away defeats from Celtic and a narrow loss to Rangers ultimately cost them the early reward of a quarter-final place. But had John McCormack not been encouraged to take his first and only penalty kick against Rangers, only to miss, then the possible draw would have pushed confidence even higher despite the reverses.

The season's biggest bombshell came with the replayed Scottish Cup match against St Mirren at Cathkin on Tuesday 28th February, 1961. Having comfortably disposed of Arbroath in the second round 5-2, Thirds had travelled to Paisley for the next.

Saints were fortunate to get away with a 3-3 draw and Thirds fans were eagerly anticipating a glory night in the replay at Cathkin.

Disaster struck with a vengeance! Thirds finished on the wrong end of an 8-0 scoreline, with their faces as red as their jerseys.

It is a fact that a certain Cathkin supporter was on a business trip that day which had taken him to Ullapool. As was this man's habit, he telephoned the Daily Record sports desk in Glasgow and, when told the result, had to be eventually persuaded that "No, the sports people had not been drinking" and "Yes, the score WAS 8-0 for St Mirren".

This tale of woe has to be believed - the Author made that call ...

Not withstanding that cup disaster, Thirds were suitably rewarded for their overall efforts when the board agreed to a tour of Canada and the USA in the close season, full details of which are provided in another chapter.

It is worth recording the playing personnel involved in this momentous season.

They were:

Robertson, Ramage, Brown, Smith, Caldwell, Lewis, McGillivray, Japp, Reilly, McCormack, Cunningham, Robb, McLeod, Davis, Clarkston, Goodfellow, Hilley, Harley, Gray, McInnes, McCool, Gallagher, Ward, McInally, Bryce, Williamson, McColl, Grant, Brimms and Denham.

Pre-Season 1961. Thirds Full Squad. ©Hi Hi Annual.
A. Harley, J. Goodfellow, J. Gallacher, D. Brimms, J. Robertson, J. Reilly, W. Horne,
F. McGillivray, W. Cunningham, L. Denham, J. McCormack, J. Bowie, G. Ramage,
G. McCallum, J. Caldwell, J. Brown, M. Gray, R. McCool, D. Hilley, G. McBain,
W. Lewis, D. Kerr, J. McInnes, F. Howley.

It may be difficult to accept but an aggregated attendance of 132,000 was officially recorded for Thirds' six League Cup games and, even allowing for the Old Firm involvement, it was an indication too of the Hi Hi drawing power that season.

We now move to the season of ignominy, 1964/65.

Some really sensational events took place, both on and off the field. It started with the club nursing the wounds of player departures and, just before the start, Thirds were faced with demands from other players looking for further assurances regarding their future.

Alas, the goals-machine of Hilley, Harley and Gray had left Cathkin for good.

As a consequence of Bill Hiddleston gaining full control of the club and deciding to make a clear out, the trigger-happy strikers were jointly sold for a reported £78,000.

Harley moved to Manchester City in October 1962 and Hilley followed his team-mate south to Newcastle United a few days later. Matt Gray eventually joined Harley at Maine Road, Manchester in the spring of 1963.

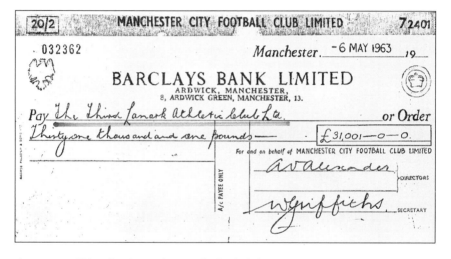

A measure of Matt Gray's worth. Note the final £1 digit.

According to the club handbook for this season, the following members comprised the board:

Chairman, W Hiddleston; Directors, Messrs White, Ross, Hough, Agnew.

Officials of the Third Lanark Development Fund refused at this time to provide any further financial support pending discussion with the board.

Early pre-seasonal discontent quickly became a "mountain of unrest", resulting in players' union boss Johnny Hughes submitting a full report to the Scottish Football League.

Consequently, a meeting was arranged between a representative of the players and the board to clear the air. It had been common knowledge that, whilst the club had taken some six weeks to put signing offers to players, they had demanded replies within seven days. Ally McLeod even to this day expresses a shocked reaction to his "free". He also confirms there was no player rebellion, only great concern over each individual's future.

The potential crisis was sufficiently resolved to allow Thirds to field this side on the first day of the season:

Mitchell; McGillivray, Davis; Little, McCormack, Geddes; Todd, Jackson, Murray, Black, Brady.

Thirds' new manager Bobby Evans, also registered as a player, did not enjoy seeing his men well beaten by Hibernian 3-0.

From day one the season's events produced a horror story. The indifferent results were being regularly fuelled by the almost daily reports of internal problems, disharmony in the boardroom and player unrest.

Thirds were relegated as a consequence of taking only seven points from the campaign. They had used 33 players and their frequent "team of strangers" had little hope of any real consistency.

The opening series of League Cup games brought two victories against Airdrie, both home and away. Three more matches passed before Thirds grabbed a precious point with a 3-3 draw at Motherwell.

One of the few highlights of the season, following another two defeats, came when Thirds trounced Aberdeen at Cathkin 4-1 with the following eleven:

Mitchell; Connell, Davis; Little, McCormack, Evans; Todd, Jackson, Baillie, Black, Murray.

Two weeks later came their only away success at Firhill. They beat Partick Thistle 1-0, with Evan Williams making his debut in goal and putting up a

Thirds Side of 1966. Connell, Baillie, Williams, Jackson, Little, A. McKay, Miller, McLaughlin, Fyfe, Kilgannon and Henderson.

wonderful show to ensure at least some celebrations amongst the dwindling fans.

Thirds had used 17 players to date and injuries were not the cause. Four more defeats followed the Firhill success and it was not until 21st November that they picked up another two points by beating St Mirren 2-1.

They were clearly flirting with disaster but even worse was to follow. Thirds went on to lose the remaining 21 league games to make it their worst season ever.

In the Scottish Cup, they travelled to Inverness to meet the local Caley and, although they eventually won 5-1, it was rather ungraciously reported in the local paper they had caught Caley on an off-day.

The next round brought Dunfermline to Cathkin and this match was drawn. The replay ended similarly and the Fifers then knocked out Thirds in the third game at Tynecastle, 4-2.

The Summer Cup brought no joy. A win against Airdrie, 5-2 at Cathkin, was their only success and Kilgannon's hat-trick was that campaign's first, although well-deserved on the day. The curtain came down on a season to forget and the long-suffering faithful thought surely now the only way was UP ...

Interesting to note the chairman's comments as they appeared in the club handbook with reference to these disasters: "Whilst the board must shoulder some blame, you will agree that falling between two stools was a possibility. Clearing off the tremendous debt left by the building of the new stand in spite of the unfortunate trend of falling gates was an achievement and kept the club alive. We have a plan to improve the facilities for fans and to strengthen the team. So, as chairman, I would beg you for your loyal support in one big effort for quick promotion to our rightful place in the first division."

Could the Hi Hi climb out of the depths of despair and return to the big time? Certainly the fans were still willing to return, albeit in much smaller numbers, to find out for themselves.

The 1966/67 season's results were almost predictable, with 13 victories from 38 starts finishing their league existence with a total of 34 points and 11th league spot in the process.

No joy in either the League or Glasgow Cups and a first round knock-out from Brechin in the Scottish Cup spelled out doom and gloom.

The following was the last Third Lanark side to take part in a competitive match.

Russell; Connell, Heaney; McLaughlin, Little, McEwan; Rundell, Craig, Busby, May, Kinnaird.

Busby scored Thirds' last ever goal in their humiliating 5-1 defeat from Dumbarton at Boghead.

Drew Busby went on to carve out a truly chequered career with a host of top clubs but his short spell in scarlet remains vividly etched in his mind and, despite it all, with some fondness.

It was business as usual off the field, with the club having moved almost permanently from the back to the front pages of the Scottish press. Predictably at one point during this season the reaction amongst players was becoming frantic, with some illuminating events shattering everyone concerned. The banner headlines of the day probably summed it all up succinctly:

'THIRDS' BOSS NAILS CATHKIN FOR SALE RUMOURS'

'PLANS TO FLIT THE CLUB'

'THIRDS LAST WARNING'

'THE CRISIS'

'THIRDS MAY PLEAD FOR CASH'

'PAY THIS DEBT OR SALE IS ON'

'CATHKIN PLAYER REVOLT IS ON'

'THIRDS' PLAYERS PAID IN SMALL CHANGE'

Small wonder manager Frank Joyner resigned mid-way through the term and the groundsman followed suit in apparent disgust.

A quite amazing and revealing incident was prominently highlighted in the press, following a game against Clydebank, in April, 1967. Bobby Shearer had replaced Joyner as manager. After the match Thirds' players, as usual, had gathered to collect their wages. Shearer found to his great consternation that they were not available but he took instant remedial action. He got hold of the gate monies and prepared the individual players' dues himself. Truth to tell one of the envelopes handed over surrendered to the sheer weight of the coins, burst open and an unidentified player was left to scoop up his wages from the floor!

Directors Hiddleston and Reilly had been in London attending an international match that day but, on their return, claimed the wages incident was simply an oversight.

In the main, the playing highlights were conspicuous by their absence but one spot of cheer came half way through the season when wee Bobby Craig returned to his first love and made a scoring impact in his debut against Alloa, with Thirds winning 3-0. Bobby, however, soon found the current Cathkin environment not exactly to his liking and quickly moved on.

Many Thirds fans will, of course, recall wryly some events which gave the Press a field day. Doug Baillie too, during his six months at Cathkin, vividly remembers a few of these Cathkin capers which are worthy of some examination.

In common with most clubs, Thirds held a pre-match talk-in but there was some extra emphasis given to the start of a game. "Don't forget", the skipper of the day was told, "if you win the toss choose to kick-off". This irrespective of any prevailing conditions. On kick-off, the centre forward was to pass the ball to either inside man, who in turn would slide it back to centre-half Baillie. Doug was then instructed to "belt the ball over the stand". Why such meticulous planning for such a tawdry tactic?

The answer is simple. At every home game the club was responsible for the provision of a new match ball and this was considered an unnecessary luxury.

So preceding Doug's "heavenly punt" a "Mr Anonymous" would be stationed behind the stand in the area of anticipated arrival and, if on course, would grab the ball and return to the referee a doctored alternative, the original having been 'filed for future use' ...

The "Missing Windows" became another sorry tale. For some weeks during the winter of 1966 several windows in the players' pavilion carried only their frames, with the glass having been cracked or removed by vandals.

This made it extremely difficult to have a bath in comfort. Baillie remembered that, on occasion, he had seen players jump into their bath in full kit in a vain attempt to soak off the game's dirt. A solution to the spartan conditions was provided by some players who, having collected flammable materials, actually started a fire on the stone dressing room floor ...

"The Frozen Pitch" tale is another extraordinary episode. One middle-of-winter Friday evening at Cathkin the players were assembled, following a request earlier in the day for them to meet. But why? The main reason brought utter disbelief, but nevertheless the directions given were followed. Apparently the club would not be able to field a full team the following day for various reasons and to avoid the censure and wrath of the Scottish League, it was considered more prudent to ensure the pitch was unplayable. With severe frost forecast for that evening Mother Nature would probably have done the needful but nothing was left to chance. The players, having been issued with pails and other receptacles, were instructed to fill them up with cold water and throw the water all over the pitch. This, combined with the natural drop in temperature during the night, did ensure that, when referee Tom Wharton arrived for the usual inspection, the ground was unplayable and the match declared off. Naturally Mr Wharton was completely unaware of the devious activity the previous night.

Incidentally, Doug Baillie's playing claim to fame with Thirds was that he was their second top scorer that season with THREE goals! Despite it all, Baillie too retains fond memories of his days in the scarlet.

The final season had brought another two personalities to Cathkin, with the arrival of new manager Frank Joyner and physio Bobby McCallum. Their sheer enthusiasm coupled with much acquired knowledge gave the players, albeit belatedly, a greater belief in themselves and, given time, there is reason to believe that, under this new team, Thirds could have prospered. But it was not to be. Following another series of revelations both men decided they had to quit despite their great admiration for what the young players were trying to achieve in an almost impossible situation.

Joyner started the season with only 14 signed players which forced him to field trialists when injury prevailed. Not at all conducive to success.

McCallum reluctantly resigned in February 1967 because of his frustration at being unable to acquire the every-day items of equipment for his job.

Having personally bought tapes, bandages and other such needs for players' treatment, McCallum felt he could no longer pay these from his own pocket.

A dedicated duo – Frank Joyner & Bobby McCallum. ©Evening Citizen.

He was not alone in feeling neglected as seasoned players such as Mike Jackson, Jim Little and John Harvey also called on the board for promises of support.

Prior to McCallum's departure, manager Joyner had received a most astonishing instruction from the directors. The use of floodlights on training nights was strictly prohibited, as was the heating of bath water for use after training.

Joyner was also familiar with another "Cathkin ball" story. There were always, in his days at Cathkin, three match balls ready for the referee's inspection. The first ball was usually an old one, but meticulously painted each Friday prior to a home game. If this ball did not pass muster with the match referee then ball number two was produced. This was likely to be a slightly newer version, not only painted but with an additional trade name added for authenticity. Assuming this ploy also failed, only then did number three came into play - a brand new ball.

Frank Joyner remembers one amusing incident concerning this. A second ball was in use in a particular match played in appallingly wet conditions.

As the players trooped off at half-time, the recently-painted trade name appeared mirrored on the forehead of one of the players. This jokingly led to players looking for assurances that their bath water did not also include "turps"!

Manager Joyner, despite a brave attempt to continue in charge, eventually and reluctantly resigned only a few weeks after McCallum. It was following Thirds' most embarrassing exit from the Scottish Cup at Brechin that Frank, having told his players, motored direct to Bishopbriggs to personally hand in his letter to chairman James Reilly.

The nightmare period continued when, some time after their Cathkin match against Cowdenbeath, the Scottish League sent the club a written warning, following a protest from the Fife club that a cheque for their share of the recent gate money had been returned "no funds".

The next week found Thirds' players demanding a meeting with directors to clear the air generally and to discuss matters like earnings "in lieu of lost wages", travelling expenses, etc. They also wanted guarantees in respect of both the floodlights and the hot water facility being available every training night.

As ever it is to easy to apportion blame for events, in retrospect, but it must be asked: How many managers would, following a training session, take five players to his home for baths on a regular basis? How many similarly would take the time and trouble to enlist the help of a group of young volunteers to line Cathkin for a match? Frank Joyner did this because of his great love for the club and the respect for the players under his charge.

It is patently obvious that over the years many, many people loved Thirds. They strove valiantly under difficult circumstances to keep the club in existence, to no avail.

Yet only a few years earlier Thirds had entertained one of France's leading clubs, Rouen, in what many hoped would have been their first of several European ventures.

The years of haggling, the internal board-room squabbles, the political intrigue, all finally led to much player unrest and the inevitable. The liquidators were called in to review club affairs and, despite behind-the-scene moves by many interested parties, the Cathkin gates were finally closed in June 1967, and the Hi Hi were no more.

In summary Thirds went out of football owing around £40,000. They had become the laughing stock in football circles. The ever-increasing arrivals and departures of managers, coaches and players, were significant.

The Board of Trade investigation as ever was particularly thorough in its examination of the club. It revealed in its report, signed on November 1967, that there had been an accelerating deterioration in the management of Thirds' affairs and its general conduct. These comments may be fairly dated from the return of Bill Hiddleston to the board in December 1962.

From April 1965 no proper books of account had been kept and this increased the task of the investigators. The report went on to say it seemed clear that Mr Hiddleston, for whatever reason, had made up his mind to secure control of the company and in this he eventually succeeded. The general picture to emerge then is that the club came to be run by him, with the tragic acquiescence of the other directors, as an inefficient and unscrupulous one-man business, with no regard for the provision of the Company Act, the articles of Association of the Company or in the interest of shareholders. Clearly excluded from any of this involvement were all persons who had ceased to hold office on or before 20th May, 1965.

Six rumour-laden years after the return of Bill Hiddleston, Cathkin Park was sold by the liquidator to a Rutherglen building firm. In 1968, James Laidlaw acquired it for a reported £35,000. Three years on, Glasgow Corporation bought the land from Laidlaw for a similar fee. To this day the former home of Thirds is used for sporting purposes. On occasion, King's Park FP have used it as their home pitch.

For the record, Bill Hiddleston died in a Blackpool hospital in November 1967. Following the club's demise he had moved south to St Anne's to become an hotelier.

So ends the Thirds story but not the romance, the colour or the drama, which constantly surrounded its life.

There remains too, the undisputed right to have recorded for posterity Thirds' deeds, covering 95 years of activity and involvement in the Scottish Football scene.

Small wonder that, even after all these years come 3pm on Saturdays throughout the season, the anger and bitter disappointment of thousands remains leaving them ... STILL SEEING RED.

Opposite: Cathkin legend Jimmy Brownlie 1911.
Over the page: Dave Hilley returns to base 1962.

THE THIRD LANARK ATHLETIC CLUB

CATHKIN PARK.

J. McINNES

Any fan can dream.

CHAPTER 4

CATHKIN CHARACTERS

There was never, throughout the years, a shortage of real personalities at Cathkin.

In an attempt to provide a flavour of the times and talents of but a few Cathkin greats, there follows a selection, taken at random, of players who graced the colours with distinction.

Inevitably such a choice is subjective. Apologies are therefore offered if any particular favourite has been omitted.

Jimmy Brownlie (1906-1923)

The best thing to happen to Third Lanark AC in 1906, was the arrival at Cathkin Park of the "immortal" Jimmy Brownlie, goalkeeper supreme.

Jimmy Brownlie. ©All Sports Illustrated Weekly 1920.

In the course of 17 years' unbroken service with Thirds, Jimmy amassed a magnificent collection of honours: 5 Caps v England; 5 Caps v Wales; 6 Caps v Ireland; 1 Glasgow Cup Winner's medal - (1908/1909); 3 runners-up medals, and 2 Charity Cup runners-up medals.

In addition his other museum pieces included 14 Scottish League awards for games against the English, Irish and Southern Leagues.

He was awarded the forerunner to today's "Player of the Year" trophy when he received a Silver Cup to mark his selection as Scotland's most popular player in 1912.

Brownlie had a remarkable memory and he loved to recall how he signed for Thirds.

In the early 1900s Celtic did not have a reserve team but they made a habit of playing "likely lads" in the hoops against provincial clubs. Jimmy had become a "travelling man" with them and got his place in a game against Peebles Rovers in a friendly. Following an impeccable 90 minutes, he was offered signing terms but, just short of accepting, Jimmy was informed by Celtic chairman James Kelly that, there was very little chance of him displacing their current keeper Davie Adams in the near future.

Jimmy then had second thoughts and, shortly after accepted Thirds' terms. With the exception of a few appearances for Morton during World War I, Jimmy proudly played for the Cathkin club for his whole career and quickly established himself without a rival in Scotland.

Brownlie often told of his debut for Thirds against Partick Thistle at Cathkin. His defence conceded two early penalties, and the resultant spot-kicks were taken by the Firhill favourite Neilly Gibson. Jimmy dramatically saved both to help Thirds win 2-1 and, not surprisingly, he grabbed the headlines from that day onwards. Thirds were only too happy to recognise his unique talents, doing what they could in a tangible way. He acknowledged the club's generosity in giving him regular increases to bring his wages in 1912 to a remarkable £11 per week. Thirds also saw fit to send Jimmy on holiday at their expense during the close season and it was reported that they had given him £30 to take "two weeks down the coast". It was a magnanimous gesture greatly appreciated by the big fellow.

Brownlie often spoke proudly of the spartan conditions which had prevailed in his playing days. The Thirds trainer would wash players down with sponges in tin, hot water baths and training consisted of three or four laps round the track. This was followed by ball practice, skipping and then a cold bath to end the workouts.

By 1921 Brownlie was idolised and included in Scotland's tour of Canada. He remembered well the heavy programme of matches, together with the very leisurely way of travel. The Scottish side visited 12 cities and finished their tour with a game against Canada in Montreal before returning home. The players were paid round £28.10/- per man, for the trip.

Jimmy Brownlie was perhaps the first goalkeeper to make his art a science when he applied a "mark" on the turf, a method the famous Jimmy Cowan used years later. It was often said that, during his illustrious career, he would put the fear of death into penalty-kick opponents, by leaving his line as the taker was preparing to shoot and making some curt comment to put the man off. It often worked!

Jimmy continued to be involved in football on his retirement from playing. He moved north to manage Dundee Hibs (now United) and had a very interesting time on the East coast.

One of his memories at Tannadice concerned a cup-tie between his club and Hearts when they held the then mighty Maroons to two consecutive draws. For a donation to his club of £500 plus half the gate Jimmy agreed to play the third game at Tynecastle. Just prior to the game, Dundee Hibs keeper Paterson was injured and, despite desperate attempts to get him ready, he was unfit to play. Jimmy, at 45 years of age and over 15 stone, came out of retirement not having handled a ball in earnest for almost seven years, to take his place in goal. Alas there was no happy ending and manager Brownlie had to pick the ball out of his own net six times.

Jimmy was well into his 80s, when he died in 1974. His contribution to Thirds was simply immense. On one of his later visits to Cathkin, he was asked about his preparation for international matches. "I worked on Saturday mornings," (his trade being a bricklayer) he said. "At lunchtime I headed for the Horseshoe Bar in Glasgow City Centre, to have my normal half-pint and a little piece of toasted cheese, the speciality of the house.

I then travelled by tram to Mount Florida, to meet up with the rest of the lads at Hampden!" Of such are memories made ...

John Ferguson (1912-1916)

The Saturday Post dated 2nd December 1916 carried the headline - 'Our sportsmen heroes - Lieutenant Ferguson - Third Lanark'.

This pronouncement heralded the sad story of the young Third Lanark rifle volunteer, the first Scottish professional footballer to give his life for his country and who was posthumously awarded the highest honour ... the Victoria Cross. John Ferguson was a real sporting hero. He was described as having a pleasing personality with no side, no swank and although university-educated, was a man with the common touch. He first appeared at Cathkin in season 1912/13 and made an immediate impact on the club officials, the fans and his fellow players.

Glasgow-born Ferguson learned the game in Rob Roy country. His first club was Callander Thistle, which he joined when still attending Callander High School.

Though inclined to be extremely serious in outlook, Ferguson was never dull and his attitude in all that he did soon had senior clubs chasing his signature.

St Bernard's had him ear-marked, following a scouting mission at a five-a-side tournament at Gartmore Highland Games, and he was duly signed.

Shortly afterwards this prolific scorer was listed to play for the Saints against Hibernian in a local cup-tie. Thirds manager Tarbert and a club director were present, along with representatives of Hearts and Newcastle and all liked what they saw of Ferguson.

How then did Thirds manage to outsmart all others to get his signature? It is reported that Thirds' manager had called at Ferguson's lodgings only to be told he was out for the night at the Glasgow Empire. Tarbert went straight there but there was no sight of his man. He left the theatre before the final curtain, came downstairs and waited outside the front doors. His tenacity paid off. He spotted Ferguson, took him for a meal and duly signed him.

Ferguson thereafter gave Thirds sterling, if short, service, making his debut against Rangers on 18th October, 1913. He scored a late consolation for Thirds but Rangers emerged winners by 4-2.

Ferguson was at this time studying for his MA at Edinburgh University and the following Saturday helped Thirds hold Hearts. Amongst the interested spectators were a large group of his "cultured" friends, who had arrived en masse to watch him play. Later in the season, Thirds travelled across the channel to Ireland and Ferguson scored one of their goals in a friendly match at Linfield against the champions. Thirds won comfortably by 4-1.

At the end of that season the club toured Portugal and Spain where Ferguson became chief "hit man" with nine goals, emphasising his eye for clinical finishing.

Jimmy Brownlie waxed lyrical about the youngster, confirming that he was liked and admired by all, both for his personal attributes and his football skills. He was a complete gentleman. Naturally Ferguson, as a dedicated volunteer, enlisted in the build-up towards the hostilities and was in uniform when war broke out. He was attached to the Scottish Rifles and quickly rose to the rank of Second Lieutenant. On a quick visit home prior to his death John had recounted his own view to friends of being most fortunate to have survived the battle so far. Sadly, not long after returning to active duty abroad, Lt Ferguson was killed in action. His conspicuous gallantry and devotion to duty was immediately recognised by his superiors, with his bravery above and beyond the call of duty being rewarded with a posthumous Victoria Cross.

Thus ended the extremely promising career of John Ferguson who, in such a very short playing career with Thirds, had made an indelible impression on all who knew him.

Neilly Dewar (1927/1934 and 1937/1940)

A very astute move by the Cathkin management in 1927 brought Neilly to Thirds. He moved south to Manchester United in 1934 also saw some service with Sheffield Wednesday and finally returned to his first love to play out a colourful career until 1940.

His name in the 1930s was synonymous with Thirds and goals, as he refused many other tempting offers to move elsewhere.

On retirement from football, Neilly went back to his native corner in Lochgilphead to work in the countryside and enjoy the peace and tranquillity so deserved. He died on 10th January 1982 and left to his thousands of football admirers fond memories of his days at Cathkin. His last "spectator" role was at Ibrox in 1945 when he was amongst a full house watching Rangers v Moscow Dynamo.

On his Scottish league debut he became an instant hit with a glorious scoring double against the English League at Manchester.

He had fond memories of his trips abroad in the dark blue. On one occasion, as the players were getting ready in the dressing-room to face France in Paris, a team-mate, Jimmy Crapnell of Airdrie, said: "this stadium is absolutely packed, we should be getting more cash for this game (£8 was the going rate)." There followed a hasty discussion which ended with the players being promised an extra 5/-. Dewar celebrated this material victory with a superb hat-trick on the park.

When he moved to Manchester, Dewar quickly introduced his new fans to his no-nonsense style of play. He married a local lass and the happy couple raised a hat-trick of sons, one of whom, Neil Junior, played for a spell with Queen's Park.

Neilly had a fund of stories on his playing career and one of these concerned "Joker" Tommy McInally, then with Celtic. In a particular game Tommy was ordered off. "To the pavilion," said the referee. "Ach," replied Tommy, "It's no a good show this week, ref. I'd rather go to the Empire."

Whilst with Sheffield Wednesday, Neilly remembers being constantly barraged with innovative training ideas. Before a cup-tie against Everton, the boss introduced to the players a little fellow complete with briefcase and bowler hat. They were told that he was a psychologist and had been asked to talk the team through the coming tie. Neilly was asked by the "psycho" to repeat three times: "I will score three goals at Goodison." Then the visiting gent confirmed that Sheffield would win the game by 4-1. With these few remarks he donned his bowler and left.

Well, it transpired that the "visitor" was right enough on the scoreline but got it the wrong way round — Everton beat Sheffield 4-1!

Neilly achieved the distinction of being Thirds' leading scorer in all but two seasons during his Cathkin spells, which was a truly remarkable achievement.

Incidentally, it was Dewar who scored the last competitive goal against Celtic great, the late John Thomson. Neilly scored the third for the Cathkin boys in a 3-3 draw against Celtic just three days before the young keeper's tragic death following a serious injury in an Old Firm match at Ibrox.

Jimmy Blair (1931-1944 and Manager 1954-1955)

Blair was signed from Royal Albert Juniors for Thirds in June, 1931. Five foot eight inches tall and weighing in at 11 stones, this inside forward gave fairly prompt warning to all that, with his strength in the tackle allied to silky passing skills, he was going to be one to watch.

His potential was quick to be realised and, in 1933, Jimmy was transformed into the most attack-conscious defender in the famous Cathkin trio of Blair, Denmark and McInnes. This scarlet mid-line went on almost uninterrupted for four seasons, providing fans with a wealth of football artistry. Jimmy forced himself into the Cathkin limelight constantly during a remarkable 14 years service.

One of his finest seasons was 1935/36 when he was involved in the Thirds side which lost out narrowly to Rangers in the Scottish Cup final. Indeed Jimmy was the only ever-present in that campaign.

He was of the quiet variety and, with the exception of season 1938/39, he was always amongst the first to re-sign. The exception was apparently

Jimmy relaxes at home with his son and daughter. ©Evening Citizen.

brought about by the club refusing to acknowledge his length of service. Happily the dispute was resolved mid-way through that season and Jimmy returned to his rightful place in the team.

Following a leg break during the latter part of season 1943/44, Jimmy Blair decided to part company with the club. It took some considerable time to recover from this nasty injury but he considered himself fit enough to play again at the start of the following season and was quickly snapped up by St Mirren. After a short spell at Paisley, he went to Shawfield where he provided Clyde with his invaluable experience.

From around 1948 Jimmy took no further active interest in the game until he accepted an approach on 25th September 1954 from the Cathkin board to return to Thirds as manager.

Blair brought to the club management the application and dedication which he had displayed as a player and, of course, was warmly welcomed by all the staff on account of his total professionalism. His reign as "Boss" was fairly short-lived and, with director Hiddleston taking more and more interest in team affairs, Blair left the club as part of an economy drive. His last game in charge was against Cowdenbeath at Cathkin on Saturday 26th November 1955, when a team of relative youngsters spiced with three recent signings from Hibernian, John Brown, Eddie Gray and Duchart, proved no match for the Fifers.

Interestingly, the match programme for that game gives great credit to director/manager Hiddleston's enterprise in obtaining the service of the three former Hibees, in addition to Jimmy Cowan, the ex-Morton and Scotland keeper. Possibly few are aware that Cowan donned a Thirds strip for five games when Robertson was absent through injury.

Jimmy Denmark (1931-1936)

During the 1930s Thirds were recognised as being an ordinary club with some extraordinary players, and Denmark certainly came into that category.

He was frequently referred to as "Thirds' beloved young skipper" because of the total dedication, enthusiasm, and skill which made him a Cathkin great.

©*Topical Times.*

106

Over six feet tall and a super fit 11st. 10lbs, this native of Glasgow began his football career with Wellshot School and progressed through the ranks to professionalism.

On leaving school Jimmy moved with his family to Canada but only for a short spell.

On his return he joined a juvenile outfit called Clydesdale, before signing for Parkhead Juniors.

Senior scouts were showing a great interest in this potential giant and amongst many others were Hearts, Aberdeen and Thirds. He was ultimately persuaded that his future lay at Cathkin, and signed for Thirds in 1931, gracing the colours with distinction for five seasons.

Jimmy quickly got his first team chance - which he took - to become one of Thirds' finest servants.

The fans were most concerned at the end of his first season - relegation being the club's fate - about whether Denmark would stay with Thirds. No deserting a sinking ship for Jimmy, who duly put pen to paper for another term. Further evidence if needed, of the well worn cliché, "playing for that jersey"!

His enthusiasm became infectious throughout the team and Thirds went on to enjoy a sparkling spell under his leadership. Jimmy was a defender but enjoyed forays into the attack. His natural and subtlety-used strength often had opponents believing they were up against the proverbial brick wall.

Denmark lost out in international recognition, perhaps paying the price of not being with a more fashionable club.

Jimmy moved to Newcastle United in 1936 but not before his massive contribution to Thirds cause in the Scottish cup final against Rangers at Hampden Park. Details of this match are given later but, when the final whistle sounded, Ibrox hero of the day, keeper Jerry Dawson, rushed to meet Denmark, and said as they were leaving the field: "Jimmy, you deserve a winner's medal for that great display."

Denmark died during the 1980s, but left forever a superb example of sportsmanship and club loyalty.

Jimmy Carabine (1934-1945 player, 1946-49 manager)

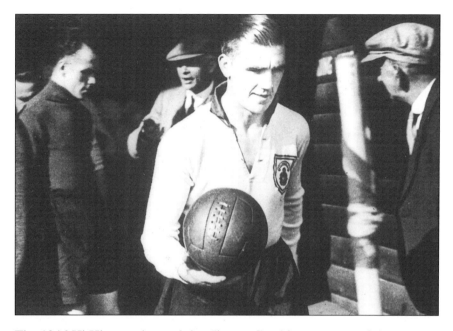

The 1946 Hi Hi annual stated that Jimmy Carabine was one of the greatest club servants of all time, reflecting on his 11 glorious years' service and anticipating his managerial service about to begin.

His love for Thirds and his role as captain and right-back over the years had fans completely accepting a total commitment and honest endeavour to win.

Carabine played more than 400 games for Thirds, during which time he was awarded 14 Scotland caps.

"Carry" guested for Hearts on occasions during World War II and was a regular member of the famous army side which included personalities such as Frank Swift, Stan Cullis and Tommy Walker.

It was a most prudent move by the Cathkin board when, after Jimmy retired from playing, he was asked to become the manager, which he did with a measure of distinction.

One extremely amusing incident connected with the "quiet man" occurred in the course of his wedding day.

Married in the morning, Jimmy checked in at Cathkin at mid-day as usual to join the squad for the afternoon game. Jimmy brought his new wife with him and, in due course, Mrs Carabine was shown to her centre stand seat to watch the game. Now the lady knew little about football but was determined to sit back and enjoy watching "her man" playing. Alas, Jimmy chose that day to fall foul of the referee. Just after the interval, Jimmy Carabine was sent off. Now "Mrs C' showed great patience for about 20 minutes. Then she turned to her neighbour in the stand to ask: "Excuse me, but when will Jimmy be back on?!"

He had a depth of knowledge of the game and players second to none. This, along with an acute awareness of their strengths and weaknesses, helped considerably to build a Hi Hi team with spirit and pride.

Carabine's managerial objective was to put Thirds among the leading Scottish clubs. Perhaps he didn't quite achieve that aim but it was not for want of effort.

Jimmy gained his initial football experience by playing through the various grades. He moved from St Joseph's Boys' Guild to Larkhall Thistle and then to Cathkin in 1934.

In addition to football, Jimmy Carabine enjoyed golf and for many years was also an ice hockey enthusiast.

He ultimately moved into sports journalism where he regularly penned match reports and football snippets in his own inimitable style.

He will remain clearly etched in the fans' memories.

Jimmy Mason (1936-1952)

The penalty inflicted on Jimmy Mason for choosing the scarlet of Thirds as opposed to the "more acceptable Glasgow colours" was the lack of international recognition, at least until 1948. Then the selectors of the day ultimately agreed he was the finest inside-forward available for Scotland. For many, Jimmy had been exactly that for most of his career.

It took the English club managers for whom Mason guested during the war to rave about this man's talents before the Scottish football powers took notice.

One such admirer was Jimmy Seed, of Charlton, who was quoted as saying "Jimmy Mason in my book is an even better footballer than the great Alex James."

Jimmy arrived at Cathkin as a fresh-faced teenager in 1936, having signed for an extremely observant manager Tom Jennings. Full credit to the astute Cathkin boss for snatching the youngster away from such clubs, as Arsenal, Rangers, Hearts and Aberdeen, to name but a few.

Mason had started his football career at school. He was a member of the Haghill Primary School team and, on scoring his first ever hat-trick received a very generous gift of 2/6 ($12^{1}/_{2}$p) from the sports teacher. Having gone through the school team ranks Jimmy surprisingly decided to watch Petershill Juniors. His brother Archie was a star for the "Peasies" at the time and ironically Jimmy enjoyed the spectator

role. Being fully aware of his abilities, however, Tollcross Juveniles chased him to obtain his services and their persistence finally paid off. Mason signed but did not remain in their ranks for long. Within a couple of months he had joined Mossvale YMCA in Paisley and this led to the man with the educated feet becoming a prime target for many clubs. Jimmy decided to go Junior and played with Cambuslang Rangers. He soon found, however, that the Juniors was not his scene, having not really enjoyed his first few games of the more physical variety. Then the real chase started. Every evening on his way home from work (he was a trainee brushmaker) Jimmy got unexpected additional dribbling practice avoiding the football scouts and managers, who gathered outside his home.

Leicester made a unique offer, to send him to their local university for further study if he would sign. Jimmy made up his own mind and duly signed for Third Lanark on 18th June 1936 at the tender age of 17.

Jimmy Mason was richly endowed with natural talent, but quickly acknowledged he could still improve his ability by being able to make more use of his left foot. Lots of training under the supervision of manager Jennings followed and paid dividends. Jimmy later paid tribute to his manager's interest for this personal attention. His eight stone frame in the early days was not built for conflict and often he himself overheard the comment from friend and foe alike: "He's far too wee." His reply was doing what he did best - to confuse all with his own brand of skilful football. During the war years Mason guested with Portsmouth and Charlton and indeed the former were specifically instructed to insure him for £5,000. The Portsmouth secretary replied to this request in the affirmative but added: "That's more than the other ten players here have in cover together." Such was Mason's worth.

Jimmy was chosen to play for the Scottish League against League of Ireland at Ibrox on Wednesday 29th September 1948, his Scottish League debut. He gave a five-star display and, considering it was his third competitive game in five days, he deserved the rave notices which followed.

The Scottish League side was: W Miller (Celtic); W Kilmarnock (Motherwell); D Shaw (Hibernian); R Evans (Celtic), G Young (Rangers), S Cox (Rangers); W Waddell (Rangers), R Combe (Hibernian), W Houliston (Queen of the South), J Mason (Third Lanark), L Reilly (Hibernian). Two goals a-piece from Combe and Reilly and a single from Houliston enabled the Scottish League to take the honours with a convincing 5-1 win.

On the previous Saturday Mason had been in Thirds line-up for the league game v St Mirren and on the following Monday he played for Thirds against Celtic in the Glasgow Cup final at Hampden. Shades of yesteryear, with the reported attendance for the Celtic game being 82,000. Sadly for Jimmy, Thirds lost 2-0, but this did not dim his sights for the Inter-League match on Wednesday.

Four weeks later - Saturday 23rd October 1948 - marked Mason's first full Scotland cap. He played in the number eight shirt against Wales at Cardiff and a superb 3-1 win followed. Jimmy stamped his indelible skills all over the match. Suddenly this "international outcast"became a Scotland regular. Several honours followed:

Full Caps: v England 1949; Wales 1948, 1949, 1950; Ireland 1949, 1950, 1951; Austria 1951; Belgium 1951.

League Caps: v England 1949, 1950; Ireland 1949, 1950, 1951.

League of Ireland: 1947, 1949, 1950.

That he was the master of the "dummy", both on and off the field, is illustrated in a recorded story concerning Jimmy when with the Scottish party at Sonning for a game against Wales at Cardiff. It was regular practice for the players to "do up" their team-mates' rooms. Mason was seen by some players coming out of a room and that was enough for them. In a gang they swooped on the room and gave it a proper "going over". Mason was nowhere to be seen when the deed was done. Later he became the centre of ridicule, and Jimmy played along with it for almost an hour, vowing revenge. He was to have the last laugh! Sure he had allowed himself to be seen coming out of a room but it wasn't his ... Imagine the surprise and shock when the pranksters discovered the room given the "treatment" belonged to none other than Chief Constable of Glasgow, one of the guests with the SFA party! Happily the "Chief" Malcolm McCulloch enjoyed the joke and took it in the manner intended.

How many players played senior football for 16 years and held this "character reference": Bookings - one; Ordered off - nil?

The biggest transfer temptation came to Jimmy Mason in 1952 with the arrival in Glasgow of a delegation from the Lazio club of Rome. Thirds had been contacted about the Italians' interest and called all parties to a secret meeting in the Adelphi Hotel in Glasgow.

The officials of Third Lanark and Lazio agreed on the transfer (no great surprise) and Mason was offered a personal signing-on fee of £4,000 with win/draw bonuses of £20/£10 respectively, and £20 per week wages. In addition a car and flat would be provided. Thirds were being given £15,000 but later upped to £17,500 ... staggering terms for the era!

A unique clause was also to be inserted if accepted:- Mason's children, Ian, Isobel and twins Archie and Alec, would be educated - without religious instruction - at a local Convent School. The transfer meeting lasted four hours, and Jimmy asked for time to talk things over with his wife Ella.

The outcome was that Jimmy rejected the sensational move to Italy and played for Thirds that weekend to resume his one-club affiliation for the rest of his career.

On 18th October 1952, Mason pulled on his beloved scarlet shirt for the last time against Motherwell at Cathkin. Following that game he was advised to retire due to severe and persistent groin injury and, at the age of 34, said goodbye to competitive football.

Not surprisingly he was given a testimonial match, on 30th April 1953, which brought out an amazing 14,000 adoring fans to Cathkin to watch a Scotland Select play Sunderland. Jimmy was eventually persuaded to "kick

Mason flanked by Billy McPhail and Billy Steel kicks off at his Benefit Match.
©Hi Hi Annual.

-off' in a game that saw Scotland win 5-0. Billy McPhail (Clyde and Celtic) scored three, with Wright and Billy Liddell getting one each. Whilst the authorities were dreadfully slow to recognise Jimmy's abundant talents and cap him much earlier, they at least accepted his loss honourably and arranged for a galaxy of talent to play in this game for him. Cathkin was graced by many stars that day, which was simply a reflection of the high esteem in which Mason was held throughout Scottish football.

The Scottish XI
Cowan (Third Lanark);

Young (Rangers),		Harrower (Third Lanark);
Scoular (Portsmouth),		Aitken (Sunderland);
	Cowie (Dundee)	
Wright (Sunderland),	McPhail (Clyde),	Liddell (Liverpool).
Henderson (Thirds),		Steel (Dundee).

Incidentally, the Sunderland team that day included the great Len Shackleton and Welsh internationalist Trevor Ford.

The event was followed by dinner, with SFA chairman Bob Kelly proposing the toast to the guest of honour Jimmy Mason. This brought an end to the playing career of one of football's immortals.

Mason died on Saturday 4th December 1971 at the relatively young age of 52. He was flying home from holiday along with his wife Ella and two friends. Just before the plane landed, Mason collapsed and despite hectic attempts to revive him he was pronounced dead on arrival in a private area of Glasgow Airport lounge.

Jack "Soldier" Jones (1937-1946)

Thanks to a technical hitch by Celtic, who had actually signed Jones on an amateur form during the close season of 1937, Cathkin boss Tom Jennings was able to step in and lure the youngster into the Hi Hi fold.

Jennings personally called at the Greenock home of Jones to ensure this lad of tremendous potential donned the scarlet for almost nine years, with only war service interrupting.

Before joining the army, Jones had played for a local juvenile team, Heatherbell Gourock, and also for Gourock FP. Strangely they considered

©*Topical Times.*

him to be on the fragile side, particularly for his role as an inside-forward.

Following early army service, he returned to Greenock where two of his friends arranged for him to have a trial game with Yoker Athletic. He played and made an instant impact which resulted in signing offers from other clubs and Jack eventually joined Morton Juniors before stepping up to the seniors with Third Lanark, despite fresh approaches from Celtic and several English clubs.

The season prior to Jones' arrival finished on a relatively high note for Thirds, although they lost out to Rangers in the Scottish Cup final. The fans eagerly anticipated the arrival of Jones having read his glowing press references.

His signing completed an inspired inside-forward trio of Mason, Dewar and Jones, with their inherent and varying talents complementing each other. The result of their first season together was the scoring of 30 league goals among them. Dewar hit 18, Jones eight and Jimmy scored his customary contribution, four (Mason, of course, was always accepted as playmaker not goalscorer). The next season saw "Soldier" netting 21 league and six cup goals and Thirds' super strikers claiming 49 league goals plus 13 in cup games.

115

In 1939 the brilliant talents of Jones, was recognised by the Scottish selectors in their choice of players for the close season tour of Canada and USA.

For interest, the full Scottish party selected was:

J Dawson (Rangers), D Gray (Rangers), B Ellis (Motherwell), J Carabine (Thirds), B. Bolt (Rangers), W Lyon (Celtic), J Dykes (Hearts), A McNab (West Bromwich), T McKenzie (Motherwell), T McIntyre (Hibernian), M McDonald (Celtic), G Hamilton (Aberdeen), A Garrett (Hearts), Jack Jones (Thirds), D McAvoy (Kilmarnock), J Gillies (Clyde), J Caskie (Everton).

Jones continued on the goals and glory trail for Thirds. The 1939/40 season brought no silverware to Cathkin but some tremendous matches took place. Jones assisted Neilly Dewar to grab 11 goals, which made him the club's top scorer, and Jones himself netted nine.

"Soldier" bettered this the following season when he became Thirds number one hit-man with 13 cracking counters.

The next two seasons found new arrival Johnny Connor endearing himself to the fans with 27 and 21 goals, the majority of which were made by Jones who himself scored 13 and 12 respectively.

The next Cathkin striker to enjoy the "Made by Jones" touch was George Henderson, who scored 24 goals in season 1943/44, with Jones notching a personal tally of 11. The final war-time campaigns of 1944/45 and 1945/46 brought Kenny Dawson into the scoring act and he led the Cathkin scoring parade with 14 and 13 strikes. Dawson was first to admit the goalmaking skills of Jack was responsible in no small measure for this scoring success rate.

During his career "Soldier" scored around 150 goals, but his "assists" would be incalculable.

War-time restrictions contributed to his dearth of caps but, in common with others in football suburbia, he may well have suffered from playing outwith the recognised "big guns".

Jack Jones (extreme left) on Board ship Bound for New York, with S.F.A. Tour Party of 1939. Thirds' Jimmy Carabine is seen sporting the snappy brim (3rd from right).

When hostilities ceased Jones was 30 years of age and, with his appearances becoming more irregular, he accepted a "free" at the end of season 1946/47.

Stranraer acquired his services and, although he enjoyed his days there, his happiest memories remained at Cathkin.

For the record, Jones' final first XI game for Thirds was against Morton at Hampden Park, on 21st August 1946. Carabine scored Thirds' goal in their 4-1 defeat. Team: Petrie; Balunas, Kelly; Middleton, Black, Mooney; Carabine, Ayton, McCulloch, Jones, Kinnear. His last game in scarlet came for Thirds' reserves against Hamilton at Douglas Park, on 20th September 1946, in a 3-2 victory, with "Soldier" scoring the third to go out a winner.

Jones did not amass many caps but achieved footballing excellence in other ways. His loyalty, commitment and unique playing style, coupled with his prolific scoring ability, endeared him to all.

Harry Mooney (1942-1955)

Harry Mooney, known affectionately as "The Iron Man", was one of Cathkin's longest-serving players.

He gave Thirds 13 years' excellent service, which was fortunate for both the club and their fans who worshipped him for his determined, enthusiastic and skilful attributes.

Mooney was 26 years old when he arrived at Cathkin and 39 when he left, still producing his own brand of total football.

He went on then to give service to Alloa Athletic and East Stirlingshire before finally retiring from the game at the age of 43. Mooney contended that his fanatical attention to personal fitness ensured his ability to play on.

Harry's other claim to fame was, along with Thirds' team-mate Jocky Robertson, he tied for the title of being Scottish football's smallest player at a mere 5' 4" tall.

©*Cassidy Kilsyth.*

Mooney signed from Bedlay Juniors and it is worth recording the reason for his ultimate arrival at Cathkin was because of a personal contact at Bedlay. Dan McGachie, a member of that club, was also associated with Thirds as a scout. He had been anxious for Mooney to move to Cathkin previously but Hearts had arrived on the scene with an excellent offer. However, a leg break to Harry ended Hearts' interest and, when he began playing again, Thirds stepped in to sign him.

A miner, Mooney's normal working week consisted of five and a half days down the pit. His Saturday schedule did not change much over the years. Harry would cycle from home to the pit some six miles away. The Saturday working hours were 7am until 11am when he cycled back to his Kilsyth home. A quick change, then on to Cathkin, taking the bus into Glasgow and tram out to the south-side ground.

The end of hostilities in 1945 saw Thirds go full-time and Harry joined the club on a new full-time contract when the sum of £12 per week with a £2 win-bonus was paid.

During the close season Mooney kept himself fit with daily solo runs over his beloved Kilsyth hills and this fitness coupled with his natural tenacity earned him the respect of friend and foe.

His two greatest personal disappointments in football were that he never ever played in a Scottish Cup final nor was capped for his country.

Some years ago, when reflecting on the modern game, Mooney said: "I am not really impressed with the outcome of the now generous wages structure and contracts. The Junior game retains a healthy spirit, with many youngsters still striving for a professional career but some aspects of the seniors leave me cold. Contracts for instance can so quickly be broken. How often do we read of a player signing for club A, the club of his dreams, before some months later becoming completely disillusioned and demanding a transfer."

Despite the more stringent applications of rules and regulations, prevailing in the 40s and 50s, Mooney remains a devotee of that system of necessary discipline.

Harry's one-time ambition was to be a Celt but this did not materialise and full credit to the wee man's steel and style that he probably performed with even more determination "if that was possible" when he faced the men in green and white.

Mooney particularly recalls one Celtic match with good reason! The Celts were comfortably beating Thirds 3-1 when Harry got involved in a chase for the ball with Willie Fernie. Both were going full pelt on this occasion but Harry denies any responsibility for Fernie tripping on the run and falling on his face. The referee obviously agreed and waved play on, much to the consternation of the Celtic fans. However, another Celtic goal pacified the home supporters and Mooney forgot all about the incident until arriving for morning service the next day at his local RC church. He was greeted rather coolly at the door and told to see a certain priest at the end of service. This he duly did, to be reminded in no uncertain terms about his one man "warfare" against Celtic players in general and Fernie in particular. Harry reminded his "accuser" in his most sincere manner that, whilst he was a good Catholic and would always remain so, a game against Celtic was no different than any other! Suffice it to say that conversation has been the subject of many a laugh since between Harry and the man of the cloth.

His real regret was the demise of Thirds in 1967 and the scandal which followed. But, not even that could detract from his love affair with Thirds.

For the record this man's amazing physical fitness saw him recover from a horrendous series of breaks during his career. Two arms, one leg and two ankles were encased in plaster at one time or another, in addition to a broken collar bone on three occasions and also cracked ribs. His Cathkin deeds were legendary and the following statistics only emphasise his fitness and dedication.

Season	-	Appearances:	Season	-	Appearances:
1942/43	-	31	1949/50	-	18
1943/44	-	30	1950/51	-	27
1944-45	-	32	1951/52	-	35
1945/46	-	29	1952/53	-	32
1946/47	-	38	1953/54	-	37
1947/48	-	32	1954/55	-	29
1948/49	-	34			

The midfield dynamo had tremendous energy and courage which, allied to his club loyalty and football skills, made little Harry a BIG personality at Cathkin.

Bobby Mitchell (1943-1949)

A multi-talented winger, Bobby joined Thirds as an amateur from juvenile club Market Star in 1943. His career at Cathkin was quickly interrupted by war service in the Royal Navy.

On demob he returned to the Hi Hi as a professional and was one of their brightest prospects. He quickly became the No. 1 personality in the side.

Mitchell was capped in 1947 against the English League and three years later played for the full Scotland international side against Denmark.

"Twinkle Toes" was a complimentary reference to his ability to work wonders on the ball. In fact a comment in one match report read: "Bobby Mitchell did everything but make the ball talk - but we're told he's working on that!"

In his day Bobby, with an educated left foot, was often called a "one-legged wonder" ... words usually echoed by frustrated opposition fans.

Goalkeepers of the day were well aware of the ferocity of his left-foot strikes. "Mitch's" inch-perfect crosses, subtle free-kicks, deceptive swerves and the sheer strength on long wing runs were all hallmarks of his skills.

He was mentioned regularly in the same esteem as Thirds greats like Dewar, Carabine and Mason, the ultimate in Cathkin compliments. Unfortunately for the success-starved Cathkin fans, Mitchell was allowed to join Newcastle United in 1949.

An interesting story surrounds his transfer. Newcastle director Stan Seymour, had travelled north to watch a couple of Partick Thistle players, who were included in the Jags side playing Thirds in October 1948. It was the amazing "Mitch" who instantly took the Seymour eye, not the Thistle players previously recommended.

Bobby's display held Seymour spellbound and three more visits were more than sufficient for the English club to put in an offer for Mitchell. Initially the Cathkin board refused their approach and, for a couple of months, nothing happened.

Sometime later Bobby hit a spell of poor form and was relegated to the reserves.

©*British Football Teams.*

That was when Newcastle came back again, with Seymour watching him play for Thirds Reserves against East Fife at Methil. Newcastle United secured Mitchell's transfer for a reported £18,000, a Scottish record at that time.

On completion of his first full season with Newcastle, the club admitted that the Mitchell transfer was just about the best bargain buy the club had enjoyed in many years.

Bobby made his Newcastle debut in the derby game against Sunderland on Saturday 5 March 1949.

His playing statistics with Thirds and Newcastle were:

Newcastle United   **Third Lanark**
League games 376   League/cup games 196
Goals scored 95   Goals scored 43
FA Cup-ties 41   Charity Cup Winner's Medal 1, 1956 (Guest)
Goals scored 18
FA Cup Winner's Medals 3, 1951/52/55

Mitchell regularly had a hard time from defenders, but this did not deter him from producing a real "Tormentor's Role", which elevated him to the football hall of fame.

Ally McLeod (1949-1956 and 1963)

Ally McLeod made his Thirds debut at the tender age of 18 on 6th November 1949.

He received pass marks on his performance but not a win bonus as the Hi Hi lost at home to Stirling Albion 4-2. From then onwards this gangly youth, who ultimately saw football service from Cathkin to Cordoba (as the Scotland team manager), became very much part of Third Lanark.

Ally eventually won over the majority of fans to his way of doing things. Not for him the orthodox but rather the unexpected. His philosophy simply was: "if I don't know what I intend doing next, then neither will the opposition..."

123

McLeod was not only an exciting and entertaining winger but a real Hi Hi fan too. One thing Cathkin supporters found out quickly: there was never a dull moment when Ally was on the ball!

"The bigger the game the better the performance" was true in McLeod's case. Manager Jimmy Carabine was made aware early on that Ally could play some and never better than when pitched against Ibrox giant George Young. McLeod took the big man to the cleaners and not too many could make this boast. George reluctantly had to confess to Ally's success but added: "His unorthodox style totally confused me." Even Thirds team-mate Jimmy Mason had been heard to say to Young, following another McLeod "roasting", as the teams left the field: "Don't worry too much, George, I play with him every week and still don't know his next move."

©Daily Record

Not all opponents enjoyed Ally's talents. Johnny Little, former Ibrox half-back and a personal friend, recalled: "I had plenty of time to study his style. He was skilful, excellent at rounding full-backs and full of running. I remember in one game at Ibrox McLeod had been giving the Blues defence nightmares. I heard Willie Woodburn mutter 'OK, enough is enough.' Now Woody wasn't known for his patience, and we knew what his comment implied. Sure enough, the next time Ally raced past George on the touchline big Willie, at full tilt, chased his target. McLeod, though, sensed the Woodburn approach and put an instant brake on his run and at the last moment dragged the ball back with him to leave Woodburn to career on over the line, flattening a linesman in the process. Ally breathed again, but was eternally grateful for his 'third' eye."

The boot was on the other foot, however, on another occasion, according to former referee Peter Fitzpatrick, who was in charge of a Thirds-Rangers cup-tie in 1954. He confirmed: "I was standing on the goal line just outside the post, during a Thirds attack, when the ball hit me and rebounded to McLeod only two yards out. Before he could shoot into an empty net Rangers 'keeper Niven shouted 'It's a goal kick' and Ally passed the ball back to him. Niven then kicked the ball out most gratefully from his hands. On the interval whistle, the Thirds captain challenged me as to why I had allowed Niven to clear from his hands. 'Because it had never crossed the line' I replied 'and was still in play.' 'You mean if McLeod had scored it would have stood?' he asked incredulously - 'Yes' I had to reply ... The skipper headed straight for young Ally and not to pat his back ..."

Cathkin games bring memories flooding back to McLeod but, strangely, it was a League Cup-tie at Alloa on 8th August 1953 which brought a real smile to his face. History was made that day when Thirds hammered in 10 goals without reply but the main purpose during most of the 90 minutes was to get Ally a goal. He had had opportunities galore and before the finish a flashing left-foot drive and a simple tap-in gave him a deserved double.

Thirds, nostalgia and Ally McLeod still walk hand in hand. He remains a Hi Hi man and had no intention of leaving Thirds but the board kindly invited him to go, explaining that Thirds needed a new enclosure and their only hope was in the transfer market. McLeod was sold to St Mirren for a reported £8,000 but moved on again within six weeks to Blackburn Rovers, with whom he carved out a superb career. He returned to Hibernian, in 1963 and completed his playing circle, by "winging" it back again at Cathkin for another year.

Ally thrived on big crowds and remembers well, in the early 1950s, regular crowds of around 45,000 to 50,000 attending games against the Old Firm.

His first game for Thirds brings a wry smile to his face. "Even if I didn't set Cathkin on fire that day someone else did!" As the players trooped off at the end of the game the stand was ablaze. The players had to grab their clothes from the dressing-rooms and run clear.

Ally emphasised the friendliness within the club at this time. "It was always a happy place," he said, and added, "people always came first and enjoyment was always well up on the list of priorities."

Ally McLeod carried the Scottish flag world-wide as international team manager but, to all Thirds' fans his world began and ended in that little corner of Glasgow's Cathcart Road.

Wattie Dick (1949-1955)

In June 1949 in the Motherwell dressing-rooms at Fir Park, after a dazzling display for Forth Wanderers in the Lanarkshire Junior Cup, manager Jimmy Carabine smartly stepped in to sign Dick for Thirds.

An inside-forward who would fight tenaciously for possession, distribute the ball intelligently and also take over the goal-scoring role himself, is worth a fortune to any club. One such man was Dick, Thirds' multi-talented capture.

The Forth lad signed when 21 years old and benefited from his Cathkin apprenticeship alongside Jimmy Mason (who wouldn't?). Eventually Wattie took over the "Maestro's" mantle to guide Thirds following Mason's enforced retirement. Motherwell, a few years later, made three ambitious attempts to entice Dick to Fir Park but to no avail.

His debut was perhaps uninspiring but remembered. He wore the colours for the first time against Partick Thistle on 12th November, 1949. Playing at centre-forward, he was slightly overawed by events, but, as Thistle won 3-0, Wattie was apparently in good company.

Thirds were still convinced they had signed a winner and,

©Hi Hi Annual.

126

following some experience gained in outings with the reserves, Dick returned to first-team duty on 25th March 1950, against Stirling Albion at Anfield, and he never looked back.

Unless injured or ill, Wattie was an integral part of Thirds.

A particularly sweet memory was a meeting with Celtic in February 1953 in the Scottish Cup, when, against all odds, Thirds held the Parkhead side to a 0-0 draw in the first game, taking them to Cathkin for the replay.

The replay was duly scheduled for a Monday afternoon when 30,000 plus fans attended.

The wintry weather conditions meant that to have the park playable, about 50 tons of sand had to be applied and the outcome was that Cathkin's "little Sahara" was only declared playable less than half an hour before kick-off.

The teams were identical to the first match but, on the final whistle, Thirds had not only knocked the much-fancied Celts out of the cup but had gone into the history books in the process! They were the first club to have beaten the Parkhead side in a replayed Scottish Cup-tie.

The scoreline of 2-1 did not flatter them and it was a dandy double from Dick that saw Thirds into the next round.

At this time Dick acquired the nickname "Moby", the explanation being his team-mates thought he was a whale of a player.

At Cathkin Dick was acknowledged as "Mr Goals". When he joined the Scottish colony at Accrington in 1955, along with team-mate Norman McCreadie, Wattie was accredited with 96 goals for Thirds.

Dick was a member of the victorious Charity Cup-winning side in 1953/54 and also played his part in the Glasgow Cup-"sharing" final with Clyde,when a draw in May 1952 enabled both clubs to hold the trophy for six months each.

By any standards, the Cathkin side of Watt's era would be considered formidable. Goram; Balunas, Harrower; Orr, Christie, Mooney; Henderson, Mason, Cuthbertson, Dick, McLeod.

Amongst his big disappointments was the "so near and yet so far" Scottish Cup run of season 1952/53.

Thirds eventually went out to Aberdeen in a replayed semi-final at Ibrox, due to a defensive slip-up. A woefully short pass-back enabled Paddy Buckley to step in and equalise in the first game, then the Dons proved too good in the replay.

Dick's prodigious work-rate and goal-scoring abilities made him a real favourite.

He played 218 games for the first XI and never gave anything less than 100 per cent.

Dick's strike rate of 96 goals says it all and explains why it was a sad day for the faithful when he decided to move on.

Promises of a benefit match did not materialise and, as Wattie felt he wanted to remain full-time and did not relish another season in the Second Division, the club reluctantly listened to offers. One player at Motherwell was definitely not sorry to hear of Dick's pending departure and hopeful of him moving out of the Scottish League altogether. That was John Johnstone, the 'Well keeper.

On two separate occasions, the keeper had been injured when trying to stop Dick volleys and the second time Johnstone was left nursing broken bones in his hand.

In June 1955, having completed six superb campaigns at Cathkin, Dick started the first of four seasons with Accrington before moving on to Bradford P.A. This completed a rather unenviable hat-trick of services to clubs who have for one reason or another disappeared from the Scottish and English Leagues.

No fault of Wattie Dick, though, who retired from active participation in football during the summer of 1963.

Hi Hi fans will not forget the tremendous contribution made by him to Scottish football in general and Third Lanark in particular.

John "Jocky" Robertson (1951-1963)

A calculated gamble by Thirds manager Alex Ritchie in December 1951 resulted in the signing of Scotland's smallest, and arguably finest, uncapped goalkeeper.

Over a period of 12 years, Jocky endeared himself to fans countrywide,with whom he had a happy knack of developing an almost instant rapport. His saddest moment in football came when he was given a "free" at the end of season 1962/63. He moved on to provide Berwick Rangers with a full season of cover before retiring from the game for good.

The "wee fella", standing only 5'4", made a remarkable debut for Thirds on 22nd December 1951 at Airdrie. He clearly remembers the various impacts made on his new colleagues when Alex Ritchie took him into the Thirds dressing room on match day to introduce him to the rest of the team.

A hush descended immediately when Ritchie announced: "Well, lads, here is your new keeper." Many muttered comments were made as Thirds players eyed up this last line of defence. Just before running out for the warm-up, Harrower and Balunas collared Jocky to ask: "How do you like to play it?", this with reference to his style of goalkeeping. Jocky replied confidently: "Everything in the six yards box is mine, and when I shout for the ball I want it, right? If anything goes wrong after that, I'll take the blame."

If Jocky's new team-mates had doubts as to his ability, they had these at least partially dispelled in a quite remarkable vote of confidence. As the players ran ©*Hi Hi Annual.*

129

onto Broomfield Park, Robertson's personal fan club from Armadale Thistle Juniors, totalling several single deck busloads, cheered themselves hoarse to encourage him on his senior debut.

Jocky, with an immaculate display, played his part in the 4-2 scoreline in Thirds' favour. No question, but this 90 minutes proved conclusively to the Thirds' fans that if you're good enough you're big enough!

Robertson's real baptism of fire though came with the Scottish Cup tie which paired Thirds with Celtic at Parkhead. Thirds held Celtic to a draw and, in the Cathkin replay, defied all the odds with that amazing 2-1 win after extra time.

Jocky starred in both games and, to all Hi Hi fans, he had arrived. Hamilton Academical were Thirds' next opponents but the Lanarkshire side had acted rather prematurely with regard to the printing of tickets for the tie. Accies had assumed that their opponents would be Celtic and had to hastily arrange a ticket reprint.

A draw at Douglas Park and a home win in the replay took Thirds into the semi-final, which was played at Easter Road with Dundee providing the opposition.

Inspired by the skills of Billy Steel, Dundee ended Thirds' interest in the cup for another year.

Thirds' back three were Robertson, Balunas and Harrower and together, over the next three seasons, they were the rocks on which so many attacks floundered. Their understanding was telepathic and Harrower was sorely missed when he later moved to join Accrington.

Amongst Jocky's fondest memories, was the club tour of Canada and America in 1961. Details of this tour will appear in another chapter but mention now must be made of his only appearance in a striker role' when he turned out at centre forward for Thirds against a CYC All Stars St Louis XI reserves in St Louis, on 30th May 1961, prior to the "big teams contest" the next day.

The team had Tom McNiven, Thirds' trainer, at left-back and Jocky up front and the wee man managed to net one goal.

Robertson remembers well the rapturous reception received all way through this tour, and it will forever remain one of his highlights. Another glorious 90 minutes in his illustrious career came at Hampden Park on Saturday 24th October 1959, in the League Cup final against Hearts.

On the day Jocky turned from Hearts fan to Heart-breaker with one of the finest goalkeeping displays ever seen. All are familiar with "Cowan's Wembley", but this was "Robertson's Hampden". Despite his heroics, the score was 2-1 for Hearts. Jockey was promised a testimonial match from Thirds and, in fact, was assured at one point that the official new floodlights-opening game, Thirds v Blackpool on Monday 30th November, 1959, would provide the perfect platform. Sadly no such recognition materialised, but Jocky continued to provide total commitment.

He fondly remembers the many battles with Thirds' "auld enemy" Queen's Park and the tremendous support this south-side pair could enlist, particularly on New Year's Day games. It was not unusual for some 30,000 to 35,000 fans to gather on the Hampden or Cathkin slopes to watch these encounters.

Jocky's memory will remain to Cathkinites, as vivid as the scarlet goalkeeper's jersey he wore in the 1959 League Cup final. This was permitted because both clubs had been ordered to change strips for the final.

Thirds wore shirts of yellow with gold bands while Hearts favoured a candy-stripe outfit.

Before retiring Jocky received at least some recognition for his loyalty when a group of shareholders, under the leadership of Nancy Scott and Tommy Morrison, held a social evening in his honour.

The grateful thanks of the Cathkin faithful to this great club man perhaps may be much belated but so richly deserved.

Dave Hilley (1958-1962)

Hilley's last competitive match was played in the colours of Scarborough, then a non-league club, when he played against Stafford Rangers on 24th April 1976 in the FA Challenge Trophy final.

The game finished 3-2 for Scarborough, with the winning goal scored in the last minute. So Dave retired with a winner's medal to complete a superb playing career.

Hilley now writes about the game he loves as the North-East correspondent for DC Thomson, and his regular reports in the Sunday Post carry the same insight and professionalism as did his footballing skills. We go back to 1958 to find Dave Hilley signing on at Cathkin. Frequently compared with many stars he really remained throughout his career his own man.

Bob Shankly was manager at Cathkin when Dave arrived. Shankly was in the process then of team building and he eventually put together Thirds' finest side in years.

Cunning as a fox in football knowledge, Shankly prepared a special plan for Hilley during his formative time with the club.

©*Scottish Football Book.*

132

To protect Dave from the full onslaught of heavy tackles, Shankly would on occasion switch Hilley to the wing. This tactic paid handsome short-term dividends because, if Thirds were behind, Hilley and Goodfellow would switch positions and the ploy often paid off.

These tactics, however, came to be well-known and Hilley soon reverted to his role of inside-forward and achieved much success.

Dave well remembers his first appearance for Thirds on a trial basis. He formed a right-wing partnership with Jimmy Goodfellow in the reserve side against Airdrie at Broomfield. He scored four goals, with Goodfellow adding two to help notch a 7-2 victory. Not surprisingly, this game led to both Dave and Jimmy being signed to join Dave's brother Ian, who had arrived at Cathkin the previous season from Pollok Juniors.

Thirds on going problem was to ensure that Dave Hilley remained happy at Cathkin, because three Scottish and two English clubs were constantly after his services. He was given a couple of opportunities to move but his fondness for Thirds won the day. Hilley started his football with Muirend Amateurs from whom he moved to Jordanhill College, training as a PE teacher.

Celtic and Newcastle United were extremely keen to sign Hilley. He was capped against the League of Ireland in 1960 and another highlight was the night he scored four goals for the Scottish under-23 side against a Second Division select.

Following that outstanding 90 minutes, he was selected for the Scottish League v English League, at Middlesbrough. A 1-0 scoreline in favour of Scotland kept an excellent record intact.

Dave was in the Thirds side which went down narrowly to Hearts in the 1959 League Cup final. His brother Ian was on the Cathkin left wing in that match, which made it one for the Hilley scrap book.

His most productive Thirds season was 1960/61, as part of the famous Cathkin forward line of Goodfellow, Hilley, Harley, Gray and McInnes. Dave played 117 league games in the scarlet, and around 45 in cup competitions.

He scored 49 goals and was one of only five Thirds players who was ever-present during the Hi Hi season of 1961. This was a great tribute to his own personal fitness.

During a wholesale clear-out of players, Dave was sold to Newcastle United for £30,000 in October 1962. He later moved to Nottingham Forest, from whom he was given a free at the age of 31.

He then decided to go abroad and, played out five fruitful years in South Africa before, eventually returning to Britain and non-league Scarborough.

Hilley's Cathkin link was severed in October 1962, but his contribution to Third Lanark will always be fondly remembered.

CHAPTER 5

THE TOURS

Thirds undertook several tours abroad, in search of friendlies and challenge matches over the years.

The amount of time and travel involved will surprise many readers and clearly Thirds played their part in introducing the finer arts of the Scottish game to thousands of football fans throughout the world.

As early as 1912 the Cathkin side visited Portugal and 11 years later they became the first Scottish club side, strengthened by some "guest players", to visit South America.

The complete official tour itinerary was:

1912	Portugal	10 days	3	matches
1921	Canada & USA	81 days	25	matches
1923	Argentine	78 days	8	matches
1931	Denmark	12 days	3	matches
1961	Canada & USA	28 days	9	matches

Portugal 1912

Thirds' first tour abroad took place during the close season of 1912. They accepted the challenge of meeting three of Portugal's top sides in the space of 10 days.

There has been little to emerge in research of this visit other than the teams, results, scorers and brief comments on the overall success. Mention in one of the early club handbooks implied the tour-playing personnel consisted of the registered players of season 1911/1912. That being the case is it likely that the following players made the trip: Brownlie, Sloan, Hill, Fairfoul, Ferguson, McIntosh, Johnston, Hosie, Richardson, McFie, Cross, McCormack, Lennon.

The results:
Vigo	1	Thirds	3
Porto	0	Thirds	2
Lisbon	0	Thirds	10

Incidentally, the above player pool was, almost without exception, the one responsible for winning through the 10-game Glasgow Cup competition only two seasons previously.

The results speak for themselves and obviously this forerunner gave Thirds confidence not only in their touring ability but for the consideration for future trips overseas of a more ambitious nature.

Canada & USA: 10th May-1st August 1921

Following the end of World War I, approaches were made to Thirds to undertake a Canadian/USA tour. Apparently a sporting journalist named Bob Watson, a Glasgow man, had emigrated to Canada and had maintained his great interest in football. He had worked incessantly to organise a visit from a club from his old country and Thirds' chairman at this time, Colonel John Wilson, was finally instrumental in accepting the challenge to organise a touring side.

The players making the transatlantic trip including guest "signings" were:

J Brownlie; R Orr; C. McCormack; W Bulloch, Partick Thistle;
J Gordon; W McAndrew; C Brown, Motherwell;
N McBain, Ayr United; J Scott; A Bennett; J McMenemy;
W Rankine, Motherwell; J Maxwell, Dunfermline Athletic;
D Thomson, Aberdeen; J Lowe, Dunfermline Athletic.

The SS Cameronia, with the tour party on board, left Liverpool on 11th May, 1921. They finally docked at Halifax on 19th May, where they were met by local officials of the Canadian FA.

The matches had all been guaranteed sponsorship and, from the list of games below, it will be clearly seen Thirds were to give full value to the supporters and sponsors in the Canadian part of the trip.

21st May:	Thirds 7	Halifax	0
24th May:	Thirds 6	Montreal	2
26th May:	Thirds 6	Hamilton	0
28th May:	Thirds 4	Toronto	1

31st May:	Thirds 7	Ottowa	0
4th June:	Thirds 3	Winnipeg	1
6th June:	Thirds 3	Regina	0
8th June:	Thirds 6	Saskatoon	0
11th June:	Thirds 5	Calgary	1
14th June:	Thirds 6	Edminton	0
18th June:	Thirds 3	Vancouver	0
20th June:	Thirds 4	Is. Nanioma	0
22nd June:	Thirds 3	Victoria	0
23rd June:	Thirds 3	Vancouver	0
28th June:	Thirds 3	Prince Albert	0
1st July:	Thirds 6	Winnipeg	1
4th July:	Thirds 7	Port Archer	1
7th July:	Thirds 3	Toronto	1
9th July:	Thirds 1	Montreal	0

Record in Canada:

P	W	D	L	F	A
19	19	0	0	86	8

It was a first-class performance, even accepting the "bolstering" of the touring party. Jimmy Brownlie and A Wilson were the only ever-presents, with the latter top scorer with 40 goals.

Thirds then left for New York on 9th July to play six games in America. On Monday 11th July, they opened their States programme against New York Celtic and won 4-2.

Two days later the players left early for Bethlehem, a three-hour train journey, where they showed no weariness with a convincing 8-1 win over a local side.

Twenty four hours later it was on to Philadelphia and a 3-1 victory. On Sunday 17th July, Thirds' met a combination of "immigrants", who put up stiff resistance before a late goal gave the Scots a narrow 2-1 win.

Next stop Boston and an easy 8-3 win against Boston United was recorded. Fall River was the next destination for the final, and hardest, match of the tour. A disputed penalty awarded by the referee to the American side enabled them to snatch a late 2-2 draw.

Record in America:

P	W	D	L	F	A
6	5	1	0	27	10

The complete record in Canada and America

P	W	D	L	F	A
25	24	1	0	113	18

Argentine: 16th May-4th August 1923

If it was thought that the Scotland side in the 1978 World Cup in Argentina had an arduous task then spare a thought for the old Hi Hi, who blazed a new trail through South America some 55 years earlier.

Not for the Third Lanark tourists the luxury and comfort of modern jet travel but in contrast the long and often tiring sea crossing from Southampton in the summer of 1923.

The club had made its first ever profit of around £350, and the board, wishing to acknowledge the achievements during the previous two seasons, were determined to reward the players by planning this trip of a lifetime. In addition the Jubilee of the club had passed quietly the previous year and, whilst they had neither topped the league or won a trophy, it was still felt the players' efforts were most worthy of recognition.

Again it was agreed, as in the previous tour, that the squad would require an injection of loan players and the full complement eventually read:

F Orr, H McKenna, R Wilson, J Walker, A Reid, T McInally, W Hillhouse and J. Mitchell, all of Thirds; "guests" were T Ferguson, Falkirk; R Orrock Alloa Athletic; W Frame, Clyde; H Rae, Clyde; J Steel, Hamilton; T Glancy, Falkirk; H Ferguson, Motherwell; and R Archibald, Raith Rovers.

It transpired that, wherever two or three Scottish exiles gathered together abroad, then there was a St Andrews Club formed. In Buenos Aires there had been such a club for several years prior to the tour taking place and, following the end of World War I, the "San Andreans" there were anxious to provide amenities for a private school for the use of young Scots. The officials of this project soon realised that a visit from a Scottish football team could well help considerably in the raising of the necessary funds. Hence the original reason behind the approach and the ultimate acceptance by Thirds to undertake the journey.

On Saturday 16th May, 1923, the tourists left Glasgow for Southampton, to become the first football "missionaries" to visit South America. From Southampton, the ship called at Cherbourg, Coruña, Vigo and Lisbon, the latter two ports reminding some in the Cathkin party of their visit to Portugal in 1912.

The first match then took place on Sunday 10th June, 1923, only 48 hours after docking in Rio de Janeiro. This followed some three and half weeks at sea and, not surprisingly, most of the players were far below their best and the side struggled to draw.

The opening match against an Argentine Select provided the visitors with many clues as to the style and temperament of the South American opposition. The red-hot atmosphere in the Palermo Stadium, with 20,000 fans screaming for victory, set the scene for the games. Football fever was high and the blazing sun did not help with the lowering of temperatures, on or off the park.

At one point in the game, Thirds had been awarded a corner-kick, much to the disgust of the locals. The reaction was instant and the pitch was soon covered in debris of all sorts. The fact that the missiles thrown included knives and live ammunition did not endear the fans to the tourists and, at one stage, the Scots walked off the park in protest. They were asked to return and complete the match, being assured that the crowd reaction was quite normal for South American fans. The Argentine Select played some attractive football but they did not take too kindly to the tough-tackling tourists. A draw was as much a "political" need as a fair result.

Thirds' next opponents were Penarol, with the South Americans winning 1-0. Fortunately there was no repeat of the crowd hostility of the first match and Penarol contained several excellent players whose ball control had to be admired. Yet the Uruguayans still resented the Scots' strong-tackling and complained constantly throughout the game.

It was then back to Buenos Aires for game number three against the Argentinos which was a side closely related to the National XI.

Thirds should have been two up at the interval before the locals took the lead early in the second half. Ferguson, in Thirds' goal, was brilliant and kept the Argentinos out with Reid managing to equalise late on.

A fantastic fight-back by Thirds enabled the Scots to beat the Provincials 3-2. Two goals behind by the half hour mark, Ferguson and Hillhouse eventually equalised and Archibald shot Thirds ahead five minutes from time. Tops for the tourists were Orrock, Frame, Steel, Wilson and Glancy.

On then to meet one of the best sides in the area, Independiente. Defensive blunders gave the local side a late victory. Their first goal is worthy of recording. Ferguson, in Thirds' goal, lined himself up to face a free-kick on the edge of the box, waiting for the double blast of the referee's whistle. But the South American player hit the ball on the first "toot" to deceive the Scots keeper.

Despite Thirds' protests the goal stood. A silly pass-back brought the locals goal number two to give Independiente a 2-1 win, McInally having shot Thirds level some minutes earlier.

The match against Southern Zone produced the biggest gate of the tour, with close on 36,000 fans in the ground. They were not disappointed when Thirds chose to produce a scintillating display. McInally said later it could have been 10, such was Thirds' domination.

The team were carried off the field as a salute from the supporters, with Bobby Archibald being voted man of the match.

The scorers were Ferguson, with a 35-yard shot, Rae and McInally, against a solitary counter from the hosts.

Thirds also won their last two matches, the first a well-deserved 2-0 win against a Penarol/Uruguay select. Earlier experiences had given Thirds a lot of answers to the Latin temperament and the Scots managed to steer well clear of trouble. Ferguson and Archibald were the goalscorers.

The score in the final game of the tour was: Argentina/Uruguay XI 1 Thirds XI 2.

Two goals from Reid and Glancy were sufficient for a comfortable win. This completed the matches in this exciting and illuminating tour. Third Lanark had been warmly welcomed throughout and had proved worthy ambassadors for Scotland.

At a farewell banquet in Buenos Aires, each member of the touring party received a gold medal from the Rio Plata Association de Football.

The attendances at the games were extraordinarily good, with an average of 30,000, and everyone agreed the Rio Stadium even then was undoubtedly one of the finest in the world.

Argentine Record:

P	W	D	L	F	A
8	4	2	2	12	8

Goalscorers: McInally 3, Ferguson 3, Archibald 2, Hillhouse 1, Rae 1, Reid 1, Glancy 1.

The only minor reservation which the players had of the tour concerned at times the extremely explosive nature of the South American fans.

Financially, though, it was a huge success and for a change the Cathkin treasurer was smiling all the way back home.

Denmark: 11th May-23rd May 1931

The Thirds party left Glasgow Central Station en route to Harwich, via the Royal Scot. From Harwich they crossed to Denmark. A total of 15 members constituted the Cathkin party, which was reputed to be the youngest club side to travel abroad with the average age of the players being 21.

Cathkins "Brylcreem" Boys relaxed at Odense, 1931. ©Christoffersen Jnr. Odense.
Squad includes: Dewar, Blair, Waugh, Simpson, J. Clark, Breslin, Lynas, McLellan, Latter.

The players' party:

Waugh, Simpson, Warden, B Clarke, Latter, McLellan, Lynas, Jack, Dewar, Blair, Breslin, J Clark, Wallace.

The board had arranged this tour as a reward for winning the Second Division championship in season 1930/31.

The results of the three matches in Denmark were:

14th May: Aarborg   2   Thirds   3
17th May: Odense   3   Thirds   7
20th May: Aarthus   2   Thirds   6

P   W   D   L   F   A
3   3   0   0   16   7

Goalscorers: Dewar 7, Breslin 3, Blair 3, Jack 1, B Clarke 1, own Goal 1.

On their return from Denmark, Thirds celebrated their promotion and their tour success by holding a grand club dance in the Dennistoun Palais.

Canada and USA: 15th May-12th June 1961

As recognition for a very successful season, a lengthy four-week tour of Canada and America was arranged. Club harmony had not been stronger for many years and the players had great respect for manager George Young and trainer Tom McNiven. It was an extremely pleased group of players who emerged from manager Young's office one evening in late April having been given details of the 28-day trip, with the match itinerary as follows:

18th May:	v	Birmingham City.
24th May:	v	Ukrainian Nations.
26th May:	v	Fall River.
29th May:	v	Birmingham City.
31st May:	v	St Louis All Stars.
5th June:	v	Birmingham City.
7th June:	v	Seattle.
12th June:	v	Chicago All Stars
13th June:	v	Ontario Select.

The complete official itinerary issued to all travelling personnel makes interesting reading and provides an insight into the tremendous preparation for the trip.

Tour Itinerary:

15th May: Assemble and leave Glasgow for New York. Stay at Hotel Paramount, 235 West 46th Street, New York City. New York to Boston - Make own arrangements.

26th May:	Leave Boston for Toronto.
28th May:	Leave Toronto for Chicago and St Louis.
1st June:	Leave St Louis for Chicago.
2nd June:	Leave Chicago for Seattle.
3rd June:	Leave Seattle for Vancouver - Hotel Grosvenor.
4th June:	Leave Vancouver for Seattle.
6th June:	Leave Seattle for Chicago.
9th June:	Leave Chicago for Youngston - Hotel Todd.

McGillivray, Robertson, McParland
(Partick Thistle) at Prestwick Airport,
1961.

Dave Hilley, Alex Harley, Matt Gray in
New York, 1961.

10th June: Leave Youngston for Chicago (Rail via Baltimore).
12th June: Leave Chicago for New York.
14th June: Leave New York for Glasgow.

Thirds' playing party, accompanied by chairman W McLean, manager George Young and trainer Tom McNiven was: Jocky Robertson, Junior McGillivray, Billy Lewis, Jim Reilly, John McCormack, Willie Cunningham, Dave Hilley, Jimmy Goodfellow, Alex Harley, Matt Gray and Dave McParland (Partick Thistle, invited as guest to replace Joe McInnes, who was unable to travel), Ian McKinlay, Bobby McCool, Jim McInally and George McCallum.

Birmingham 1 Thirds 4

Thirds opened their tour with a resounding 4-1 win against Birmingham City. This was a real goal-hungry Hi Hi in a match billed as a preliminary

144

The "Tourists" board a plane for trip to USA, May 1961. Included in this Group are
Trainer McNiven, Dave McParland, Gray, Reilly, McLeod, Goodfellow, McCormick,
Lewis, Hilley, Robertson, McCallum. ©Beaverbrook Newspapers.

to the international New York Soccer Tournament. Dave Hilley was on top form, with his amazing balance and attacking skills bewildering the opposition time and again. Harley, Reilly and Jocky Robertson played well, as did Dave McParland once the Thistle man got to know his new team-mates. Thirds opened the scoring in 21 minutes. Hilley collected a slick Reilly pass before rounding the keeper to slot the ball home. Birmingham soon equalised but, just before the interval, Thirds shot ahead. Again Alex Harley finishing off a great one-two with Hilley by leaving the keeper helpless with a 15-yard rocket shot.

Goodfellow made it three on the hour and a quite fantastic Lewis solo effort ended with an unsaveable 30-yard drive for number four.

The match programme indicated that the Scottish v English clash was the opener to a double header. The other game to be played was between Besiktas (Turkey) and Karlsruhe (West Germany).

The programme introduced Thirds as follows:

"Third Lanark of Glasgow, Scotland, were the surprise team of the year. They are managed by George Young, Scotland's greatest international player. Third Lanark are dubbed the Hi Hi. Their famous manager has moulded his team into a confident combination, sure to please the American audience". They certainly did just that against 'Brum', with Bertie Auld (later to return to Celtic) in the English side!

Ukrainian Nations 1 Thirds 2

The match against Ukrainian Nations was in real danger of being abandoned due to the pitch invasion of the local supporters. It took a detachment of burly Philadelphia police to clear the park when the Ukrainian centre-forward was sent off after only eight minutes. This player virtually attacked Billy Lewis and left the referee with no alternative. Probably the fact that the Ukrainians were current American champions and had been undefeated for three years had something to do with their reaction, looking as though they were determined to win at all costs.

Dave Hilley again got rave notices for his overall contribution and a Goodfellow goal along with another from Harley were too much for Ukrainians who got a consolation effort mid-way through the second half.

146

McGillivray, Cunningham and Robertson were other top Thirds men in an excellent win.

Fall River 0 Thirds 3

The three Cathkin musketeers, Hilley, Harley and Gray, with a goal each, produced the scoring fireworks and provided the local fans with a feast of good attacking football. Reilly and Cunningham, in midfield, set up numerous scoring chances and at the back keeper Robertson and his solid defence were seldom troubled.

Fall River were not of the standard of the Scottish First Division but this 90 minutes gave Thirds a chance to bring in McKinlay and McCool, who enjoyed the experience and showed their potential.

Birmingham 3 Thirds 2

Thirds faced much stronger opposition in a return match with Birmingham City. The English side gained ample revenge with a good win. Hilley and Gray scored for the Scots but these were cancelled out as Brum notched three, the result of some dreadful defensive errors.

There was a bit of sting about this game, with Birmingham all out to prevent their comprehensive defeat of their first meeting. No real nastiness, however, was allowed to creep in thanks to a very good referee.

St Louis All Stars 0 Thirds 3

St Louis All Stars gave Thirds a very warm welcome and stated that the St Louis side were proud to be associated with this renowned Scottish team. It was a real honour to have Thirds' star-studded line-up on St Louis soil and to also meet their famous manager George Young.

Thirds did not entirely allow this "classic introduction" to affect their play and an impressive 90 minutes, laced liberally with goals and excitement, gave the fans full value. Hilley scored a double and, inevitably, Harley got the third.

Birmingham 1 Thirds 1

A "decider" between Thirds and Birmingham was played in a most sporting, yet competitive, manner. The teams were given a tremendous welcome and, having already faced up to each other twice within a couple of weeks, knew each other's style. It became very much a cat-and-mouse affair, with Birmingham content to hit on the break. The Englishmen scored early in the game but Hilley equalised in the second half. A draw was just about right.

Seattle All Stars 0 Thirds 9

The match against Seattle All Stars took place in the local High School Memorial Stadium, grand premises indeed.

Readers will, I am sure, be both interested and amused to learn that the match programme took the opportunity of introducing the game of football to the spectators as follows: "What is Soccer: It is an athletic event to which all people may compete on an equal basis. Race, creed and size are unimportant as the most treasured asset of a qualified footballer is an active brain where by he must concentrate for himself." Surely a unique and unprecedented description!

The game itself was a non-contest, McCool and McCallum replaced McCormack and Goodfellow, against a compilation of rather subdued veterans. The Cathkin boys turned on a real exhibition 90 minutes, showing their considerable repertoire of skills to a delighted audience.

Gray netted three and Hilley and Harley came up with doubles. The "stand-ins" McCool and McCallum ended the scoring to make it 9-0. The Thirds defence was rarely tested and really this was more of a public relations exercise than a serious contest.

Chicago All Stars 2 Thirds 8

It was back to Capone country and Thirds brought with them a steady supply of shooting boots.

The final week of tour began with a match against the Chicago All Stars. A thrilling display of all-out attack was the order of the day. Thirds scored eight times and could have well gone into double figures.

On this occasion Thirds were introduced to the fans as the team with most "booterage" in the Scottish soccer league and so it proved. Thirds scorers were Gray 3, Hilley 1, Harley 1, McCool 1 and Goodfellow 2 as they ran out easy winners.

Ontario Select 2 Thirds 8:

Thirds blitz of the Chicago All Stars ensured a capacity crowd turned out for the match with Ontario Select. The Hi Hi struck another blow for Scotland with a repeat of the previous eight-goal scoreline. Yes, sixteen goals in the space of two games in 24 hours - not at all bad! Matt Gray even bettered his hat-trick with a nap hand of goals this time and was given support with goals from Hilley, Harley and McInally.

Tour Record:
```
P  W  D  L  F   A
9  7  1  1  40  10
```

Goalscorers: Matt Gray 13, Dave Hilley 10, Alex Harley 8, Jim Goodfellow 4, Billy Lewis 1, McCool 2, McInally 1, McCallum 1.

In every sense, on and off the field, the tour was exceptionally successful.

Thirds had travelled some 13,000 miles, playing nine games. The Cathkin camaraderie was tremendous and the club had been great ambassadors for Scottish football.

An incredible statistic to emerge at the completion of the tour was the actual numbers of different nationalities which Thirds had faced in opposition. In addition to Canadians and Americans there were players from Portugal, Lithuania, Germany, Poland, Ukraine, Hungary and Finland also playing on the other side of the Atlantic.

Manager George Young commented: "This tour was one of the greatest things to happen to Third Lanark. It gave the players a real chance to get to know each other and gave them a prestige boost as well. The team got excellent results and this must help the players' confidence for the coming season."

Unfortunately, for every high there follows a low, but it would have taken a real clairvoyant to forecast the unrest amongst players and management to emerge during the following season.

Thirds were publicly and officially applauded for their enterprise, enthusiasm and drive, enabling them to complete a tour of such grandiose proportions so efficiently and professionally.

Jocky Robertson's daughter Heather is thrillled with her American gift in addition to having "Daddy" back home.

CHAPTER 6

GAMES TO REMEMBER

The season 1930/31 will remain clearly etched in the minds of Cathkin fans as being one of their finest. In the Scottish Second Division come the month of March, Thirds' promotion drive had intensified as they faced the final run-in.

The reports on two games detailed below will certainly illustrate the tensions, frustrations and ultimate success surrounding the Cathkin challenge.

Raith Rovers 3 Thirds 1; league; 14th March, 1931.

Raith: Leckie; Bell, Batchelor; Beath, Hoggan, Sharp; Panther, McLaren, Jarvis, McKenzie, Galloway.

Thirds: Waugh; Simpson, Warden; B Clarke, J Clark, McKellan; Lynas, Jack, McPherson, Blair, Breslin.

Thirds, the present Second Division leaders, received a nasty shock at Stark's Park when they were defeated by Rovers, who at the same time greatly enhanced their own chances of promotion, with the two valuable points.

The game was disappointing, and at one time it was Raith's 10 against Thirds' eight men. The Cathkin side lost the services of Jimmy Blair, sent off following an incident with Raith's Hoggan who was also given his marching orders. Later, both John Clark and Lynas were carried off injured and did not return.

After Rovers had taken the lead, Thirds became desperate to reach level terms and tempers again became frayed during the second-half.

Both clubs were going strongly for promotion and clearly they were both over-eager for a result.

At the beginning, Thirds looked the likelier lot but Raith slowly came into the game and carried out a series of dangerous raids. Jarvis opened Raith's account and Batchelor made it two with a penalty.

Breslin brought Thirds back into things with an excellent long-range effort but McLaren, late on, sealed it for the homesters.

Despite their handicap of playing with only eight men, Thirds' back lot were first class. B Clarke, Jack and Breslin were best of the others. McPherson, deputising for Dewar, was disappointing.

Thirds 3 Bo'ness 1 - 11th April, 1931, final league match of the season.

Thirds: Redford; Simpson, Warden; B Clarke, Latter, McLellan; Brown, Jack, McPherson, Blair, Breslin.

Bo'ness: Fraser; Sneddon, Gray; Lumsden, Fagan, McLaren; Anderson, J Aitken, Taylor, Heeps, Pratt.

The crowds rolled up to Cathkin to celebrate the club's promotion, already assured in a quite remarkable campaign.

Third Lanark started this match as though they would swamp lowly Bo'ness. They were sprightly, powerful and incisive in attack. Thirds' debutant Brown, at outside-right, gave Fraser an early chance of bringing off a fine save. Then Blair shot over from close range - all this within the opening three minutes.

In four minutes Blair opened the scoring when he finished off a combined run with Breslin. Anderson gave Redford a handful early on which might have brought an equaliser but it was all Thirds. McPherson missed an easy chance to increase Thirds' lead and even giant defender Latter had several shots on goal during the first half.

Yet Thirds forwards were really having an off day, although Breslin took some pressures off his colleagues when he made it two just five minutes after the interval.

Blair added number three when he hit home a Brown shot on the rebound and Taylor secured a consolation goal for Bo'ness.

Great celebration followed at the final whistle with most of the Cathkin players being carried off shoulder high by the ecstatic home crowd.

Thirds had achieved promotion and were back in the top division. They had lost only four games in this campaign and had scored an amazing 107 league goals in the process, a club record which still remains their all-time best scoring feat. It transpired that man of the match "Brown", was actually a trialist. His real identity was Alex Mehaffy, of Dennistoun Parish Church, who not surprisingly was signed up immediately after this game.

Thirds 0 Rangers 1; Scottish Cup final; April 1936; attendance 88,859.

Thirds were expected to turn up at Hampden purely to make up the numbers. They had struggled in the semi against Second Division Falkirk and it was 31 years since the Cathkin side had last won the cup.

Rangers, on the other hand, were going strongly in the league and looking for a hat-trick of Scottish Cup wins.

Thirds: Muir; Carabine, Hamilton; Blair, Denmark, McInnes; Howe, Gallacher, Hay, Kennedy, Kinnaird.

Rangers: Dawson; Gray, Cheyne; Meiklejohn, Simpson, Brown; Fiddes, Venters, Smith, McPhail, Turnbull.

Rangers opened strongly and a long ball out of their defence reached Jimmy Denmark. Just as the big defender was about to clear, the wind swirled the ball right off his foot. Denmark was left stranded and so too was Jimmy Blair, who could only watch in agony as Bob McPhail raced in to collect the ball, run in on goal and score with ease. Rangers were ahead in only two minutes! Thirds were stung into retaliation and only a combination of desperate defending and magnificent goalkeeping by Jerry Dawson kept them out.

Thirds Cup Finalist, 1936
T. Jennings (manager), J. Blair, J. Denmark, R. McInnes, R. Muir, J. Carabine,
R. Hamilton, J. Nelson (trainer), D. Smith (assistant trainer), R. Howe, P. Gallacher,
G. Hay, R. Kennedy, A. Kinnaird. ©Daily Record.

In 15 minutes Fiddes was injured and became a passenger for the remainder of the game. It was Thirds' big chance - but they failed to take it.

With Rangers having effectively only 10 fit men, Thirds were confident of grabbing an equaliser on the resumption, as they attacked furiously. For the next 45 minutes, the fans watched the sight of Rangers being put on the rack. Thirds piled on everything, with even their full-backs, Carabine and Hamilton, testing Dawson with raging shots. A close call, though, in 60 minutes. Dawson let a Hamilton lob pass him, thinking it was well wide, but the ball again swirled and the keeper had to make a furious late lunge to elbow it past the post to safety. Still the pressure went on. The Rangers defence was very strong and, although Meiklejohn and Simpson had lapses on several occasions, Dawson, sadly for Thirds, remained majestic throughout.

With just seven minutes left, Thirds' chance of a lifetime arrived. Kennedy pounced on a loose ball and, from all of 20 yards, released a vicious drive.

Surely a goal all the way and Thirds were almost already congratulating the "scorer" when Dawson leaped and twisted his body in mid-air to dive on to the ball and push it to safety. That was the end for Thirds.

Thirds' players and fans alike were left wondering why Jerry Dawson, had chosen this game to perform miracles. Dawson gave one of the greatest displays of goalkeeping seen on the famous pitch. It did not prevent them shaking hands at the finish, with Thirds' Jimmy Denmark remarking to Dawson: "Jerry, you should be given all 11 medals."

The road to the Final:

1st Round:
Thirds 2   Hearts 0
2nd Round:
Leith Athletic 0   Thirds 2
3rd Round:
Thirds 8   Dumbarton 0
4th Round:
Morton 3   Thirds 5
Semi-Final:
Thirds 3   Falkirk 1
(Tynecastle)

Rangers 1 Thirds 0; Glasgow Charity Cup, 1st Round; 2nd May, 1936.

All expectations of another close game as a sequel to the recent Scottish Cup final between the sides were shattered when Thirds appeared without their star defenders Carabine and Denmark, both out through injury.

1936, C.F. Action in Thirds Goalmouth – Note jam packed terraces. ©Scottish Football Book.

155

Rangers fielded their cup-winning side, except for forced changes on each wing. They played Ross, ex-Airdrie, at outside right and Kinnear on the left.

Rangers: Dawson; Gray, Cheyne; Meiklejohn, Simpson, Brown; Ross, Venters, Smith, McPhail, Kinnear.

Third Lanark: Muir; Rhodie, Hamilton; Blair, Black, McInnes, Morrison, Gallagher, Connor (Airdrie), Howe, Kinnaird.

Rangers did not play particularly well but did enough for another narrow win. Thirds on the other hand were unfortunate not to score on at least three occasions, but again it was not to be their day. Johnny Connor hit two shots on goal that had Dawson beaten, but the first screamed inches past the post and the second hit the woodwork and rebounded into the keeper's arms.

A McInnes effort mid-way through the first half dipped unexpectedly only to hit the diving Dawson on the head and bounce to safety. Then came the solitary goal, hotly-disputed by Thirds. Ross looked to be standing in an offside position when he took a Kinnear cross in his stride to beat Muir close in. Rangers were through to meet Celtic in the final.

Thirds/Queen's Park Select 1 Silesian Select 2; Challenge Game; 23rd October, 1946.

Thirds/Queen's Park XI: Hamilton (Queens); Carabine (Thirds), Kelly (Thirds); Letham (Queens), Whigham (Queens), Harnett (Queens); McCulloch (Thirds), Ayton (Thirds) Aitken (Queens), Mason (Thirds), Mitchell (Thirds).

Sir Hector McNeil, Lord Provost of Glasgow, welcomed the visitors in the match programme.

"I am of the opinion that, if the nations of the world could meet oftener on the football fields, then much good work would be accomplished in the wider sphere of life."

Playing in the scarlet of Thirds, the Select attacked from the kick-off but found the Poles a difficult team to conquer. To date in their tour they had been narrowly defeated at Dundee, but had beaten Morton and Ayr United in subsequent matches.

A lovely goal from Ayton gave the Scots hope, but a couple of quick counters put the visitors ahead.

The star of the game was Brom in the Silesian goal, stringing together a series of superlative saves.

Despite some excellent leading up work by Mason and Ayton, the Scots managed to miss at least two great chances of equalising and the visitors took their deserved plaudits.

Thirds 4 Rangers 1; Glasgow Cup, Semi-final; 7th September, 1948.

Thirds: Petrie; Balunas, Kelly; Mooney, Barclay, Harrower; Staroscik, Orr, Stirling, Mason, Mitchell.

Rangers: Brown; Young, Shaw; Little, Woodburn, Cox; Waddell, Thornton, Williamson, Marshall, Duncanson.

Rangers got a double dose of their own medicine at Cathkin before an amazing 39,278 crowd. The usual Ibrox winning ingredients of man- to-man passing and clinical finishing were transferred to the Hi Hi. They produced a quite excellent 90 minutes to destroy the Light Blues and book a final place against Celtic.

The final scoreline did not flatter Thirds. Indeed, if striker Stirling had taken the numerous scoring chances which came his way, it could have been even more embarrassing for Rangers.

Woodburn, usually so reliable, even gave his own keeper a final shock when, in panic, he sliced a Staroscik cross into the path of Stirling and the Thirds man scored goal number four with ease. Orr scored for Thirds in 40 minutes when Bobby Mitchell left both Little and Young stranded in a mazy run on goal. He finally touched the ball into the path of Staroscik and the Pole floated a perfect ball into the area for Alan Orr to head home. In 68 minutes Stirling got number two from another Staroscik service, and Orr again was on target for the third, waltzing past Cox to beat Brown.

Then came the fourth and the 'Gers were out. Thornton's goal was the sole consolation for Rangers.

Thirds were left contemplating the final against Celtic but, alas, soon came down from the lofty heights when the Parkhead side had a comfortable 3-1 win.

Thirds 2 Aberdeen 1; Scottish Cup, first round; 22nd January, 1949.

This was the club's first official "all-ticket" match. Although 40,000 tickets were printed, only 200 had been sold in advance - yet the attendance was recorded as 22,744, with fans choosing to pay at the gate on the day.

Thirds: Fraser; Balunas, Harrower; Orr, Barclay, Mooney; Henderson, Mason, McCulloch, Staroscik, Mitchell.

Aberdeen: Johnstone, McKenna, Ancell; Anderson, Thomson, Harris; Rice, Hamilton, Williams, Pearson; Hather.

Thanks to the uncharacteristic hesitancy of "Gentleman George" Hamilton with only three minutes of this tie remaining, Thirds were let off the hook, to go into the next round draw. Hamilton, in complete isolation and with only Fraser to beat two yards out, stood transfixed. Not so young Fraser, who took the chance to dive out and sweep the ball away from Hamilton's toes.

A Hamilton header had put the Dons in front, but with only three minutes until the interval Thirds equalised through McCulloch. Henderson had beaten three defenders in a wing run and his pin-point cross was met powerfully by big Adam and the ball roared into the net. There may have been some disputed decisions during a torrid second half, but none whatsoever about the winner for Thirds. Starry met first-time a Henderson corner kick and his bullet shot left Johnstone helpless.

Dons could feel cheated on account of their outfield superiority. Three times wee iron man Mooney blocked scoring efforts and Orr actually kicked the ball off the line.

Thirds 1 Reading 2; Festival of Britain Trophy; 14th May, 1951

Thirds: Petrie; Balunas, Archibald (Dundee); Adam, Samuels, Aitken; Henderson, Dick, Peat (Partick Thistle), McCall, Bradley.

Thirds began in confident style and it was no surprise when they raced ahead in only 11 minutes. Peat started the move when he took the ball through a packed defence and passed it to Dick. His shot was blocked but Peat hit the rebound goalwards only for the keeper to block it yet again. This time Henderson, running in, made no mistake as he picked his spot.

A bad mistake by George Aitken let Edelston score with a close range effort and the next minute saw Reading take the lead. Left winger Bainbridge beat Petrie with a crisp finish to a super solo run.

Despite almost non-stop attack, Thirds could not again penetrate the visiting defence, although Dick, McCall and Bradley came close late on.

Alloa Athletic 0 Thirds 10; League Cup; 8th August, 1953.

Thirds: Robertson; Balunas, Harrower; Docherty, Forsyth, Mooney, Wilson, Henderson, Dobbie, Dick and McLeod.

From the start it was evident Thirds were in the mood. Inside men Dick and Henderson worked in close harmony to set up scoring chances for Dobbie and McLeod.

They opened the scoring in seven minutes through Dick, who took a defence-splitting pass from McLeod to beat the Alloa keeper.

By the interval Thirds were three ahead with Dobbie and McLeod adding to the score.

On the resumption a glorious Dobbie hat-trick made his personal tally four, a Henderson double and another two from Dick and McLeod brought the amazing total to 10.

The final 15 minutes saw Thirds play some exciting one-touch football, with McLeod, Dobbie and Dick coming close to increasing the final tally. Poor Alloa simply had no answer on the day.

Thirds 1 Rangers 0; Glasgow Charity Cup, Final; 7th May, 1954.

Thirds: Robertson; Balunas, Phillips; Kennedy, Forsyth, Harrower; Barclay, Muir, Kerr, Dick, McLeod.

It took a superb outfield move involving four Thirds players to break the deadlock and provide the game's solitary goal, to take the cup to Cathkin.

A real pulsating battle saw a goal worthy of winning the cup between two quite outstanding teams. In 69 minutes Phillips sent a wing pass to Wattie Dick. He slipped the ball on to McLeod and Ally laid it on the proverbial plate for Kerr to smash home the winner from close range. Rangers were stung into retaliation but simply could not get the better of the Cathkin defence, with Jocky Robertson inspired in goal.

Thirds 9 Ayr United 0; League; 9th December, 1954.

Thirds: Bickerstaffe; Balunas, Phillips; Kennedy, Forsyth, Muir; Brolls, Miller, Dick, Armstrong, Barclay.

Thirds experimented with defender Barclay on the left-wing, and he had a field day. Barclay provided a spark of genius and, with fellow forwards Dick and Armstrong, had Ayr reeling under a three-man demolition job.

The floodgates opened in five minutes, when Wattie Dick sent a powerful header into the net from a Barclay cross.

Silver Ware at Cathkin. Thirds line up pre season along with Charity Cup won on the 7th May 1954.

Eleven minutes later Brolls, finished off a superb outfield move between Barclay and Miller to put Thirds two-up, and before the interval a Dick double, Barclay and Brolls made it six for Thirds. In the second-half a great double from Miller and Dick's fourth took the tally to an incredible nine.

Thirds 4 Partick Thistle 2; Glasgow Charity Cup, Final; Hampden Park; 12th May, 1956.

Thirds: Robertson; Smith, Gordon; Kennedy, Brown, Docherty; Dallas, Craig, Wark, Broadis, Mitchell.

Thistle: Smith; Kerr, Gibb; Harvey, Davidson, Brodie; Thomson, Wright, Sharp, Crawford, Ewing.

Credit where it is due and, on this occasion, no-one would have objected if an additional medal had been struck for Bill Hiddleston for his enterprise in obtaining on loan three guests, Tommy Docherty, Ivor Broadis and Bobby Mitchell, and his inspired signing of the cheekiest wee bundle of footballing mischief seen since maestro Jimmy Mason hung up his boots, Bobby Craig.

Bobby scored the final goal in a superb 90 minutes and his display along with Broadis in what is now called midfield, was inspirational. Mitchell netted the first Cathkin goal, when he sent home a vicious volley, following fine outfield play between Craig and Dallas. Davidson equalised within a few minutes and the Jags began to assert themselves. It was no surprise then when a Crawford through ball reached Sharp who shot Thistle ahead. Dallas and Wark with a couple of fine goals again gave Thirds the lead before the final Craig counter had the Thirds fans ecstatic.

A real day to remember for all Cathkin fans in one of the most attractive contests seen all season.

A wee magician, Bobby Craig. ©Hi Hi Annual.

Thirds 1 Hearts 2 Scottish League Cup, Final; 24th October, 1959.

Hearts were stunned. The faces of their players were glum, in vivid contrast to their opponents. Why? Because in the second minute of this game, Thirds had opened the scoring. For the Hi Hi it was a real rhapsody in gold, the colour of their new strip, worn for this the biggest occasion in Cathkin's history for at least 50 years.

Joe McInnes, on Thirds' right wing, accepted a pass from McCallum. He left two defenders stranded before lofting the ball into the goalmouth. Hearts keeper Marshall rose confidently to grasp the ball but a combination of late swirl and sun in his eyes saw him miss, and the ball landed behind him on the line. Ever sharp Matt Gray had only to tap it home. Perhaps it was a gift, but Thirds had made a sensational start. No wonder the Cathkin fans cheered themselves hoarse. Holders Hearts were clear favourites and their stylish play was the envy of most sides.

The Hi Hi open the L.C.F. Scoring – as the ball drops over Marshall.

Hearts attacked relentlessly following the early setback but, as time wore on, it seemed that they would never equalise, particularly with the diminutive Jocky Robertson immaculate in the Thirds goal.

Not for many a day had Hampden witnessed such goalkeeping brilliance, as Jocky brought off a string of wonder saves from Kirk, Thomson, Young and Smith. It seemed that there was no way to beat this little giant. Thirds were perfectly content to hit on the break and the Edinburgh fans held their breath each time the mercurial McInnes got the ball. The winger was having a field day and Bobby Craig almost snatched a second, while Matt Gray was only inches out with a close range shot.

In the second-half, tension built up as Hearts mounted raid after raid on Thirds' goal. Hearts forced three corners in two minutes. Brown headed a Hamilton shot off the line, Young headed the ball against the post and Smith hit a rocket from 15 yards, brilliantly parried by Robertson. Even Hearts fans had started to believe the cup had Thirds' name on it.

Suddenly the Edinburgh boys' luck turned and Thirds ran out of it. In the space of a minute Hearts cracked home two goals and, ultimately, they ran out winners. Hamilton started a wing run and released a vicious 25-yarder. Robertson saw the shot coming but unfortunately the ball took a wicked deflection off a Thirds defender and beat the keeper all ends up.

The winner came in the next Hearts attack. Young picked up a loose ball and raced in on goal. McCallum was deceived by a shuffle to let Young calmly beat the advancing Robertson with a crisp finish. Thirds then switched wingers, trying to inject more fire into their play, and McInnes almost equalised with a superb free-kick.

Sadly, even the heroics of Jocky Robertson failed to bring the cup to Cathkin. It went east to Edinburgh to make it a heart breaking day for all Hi Hi fans.

Thirds: Robertson; Lewis, Brown; Reilly, McCallum, Cunningham; McInnes, Craig, D Hilley, Gray, I Hilley.

Hearts: Marshall; Kirk, Thomson; Bowman, Cumming, Higgins; Smith, Crawford, Young, Blackwood, Hamilton.

Thirds 3 Blackpool 2; Official Opening of new Cathkin Floodlights; 30th November, 1959.

Thirds: Robertson; Smith, Caldwell; Reilly, Cosker, Cunningham; McInnes, Goodfellow, Rankin, Gray, Fraser.

Blackpool: Farm; Armfield, Martin; Hauser, Gratrix, J Kelly; Kaye, Paterson, Charnley, Durie, Perry.

Recently-signed Bobby Rankin, ex-Hearts, led the Cathkin attack and gave a personal performance to suggest strongly he could well be the answer to Thirds' recent lack of goal power, despite not being on the score sheet himself. A 12,000 crowd watched Thirds ultimately emerge victorious against a very strong Blackpool side. The victory, it was hoped, would give them new heart and confidence, two ingredients sadly lacking at that time.

Robertson made a couple of excellent saves in the first 10 minutes and this brought a measure of security to the defence. In 14 minutes, Goodfellow scored the opener when a Rankin through ball split the visitors' defence and left Jim with a simple task to beat Farm. The English side equalised in 30 minutes with Durie smashing an angular drive well out of Robertson's reach.

Thirds, however, regained their lead within five minutes when Gratrix brought down Fraser, and, from the resultant penalty, McInnes scored.

On the resumption Thirds lined up with three changes: Ramage replaced Robertson, Moles came in for Cosker and Ian Hilley substituted for Fraser.

Sub Ramage then saved Thirds by brilliantly stopping a Perry shot with only 20 minutes left. But, minutes later, Blackpool equalised for the second time with a Charnley close-range drive. Then Cathkin erupted to acknowledge another McInnes-Gray master move. Matt's perfect leap allowed him to meet a McInnes cross at the far post and Farm was helpless.

Thirds 4, Petach Tikva 0; Friendly; 1960.

The champions of Israel were completely overwhelmed by a most competent Cathkin side. An encouraging 6,000+ crowd saw the visitors squander some early chances but ultimately they were well beaten.

In the usual Glasgow downpour - perhaps the Israelis missed the sunshine - Thirds looked much fitter and faster.

Thirds used their full player pool in this challenge game and second-half substitutes Ramage, Brimms and Horne provided an interesting variation in tactics.

In five minutes Alex Harley opened the scoring with a well struck 15-yard drive. Robertson was then called into action to save, at the second attempt, a blistering drive from Kaufman. Matt Gray nodded Thirds two ahead from a perfect Goodfellow cross in 26 minutes and just on half-time he added number three. The fourth goal was a real gem in build-up and execution. Gray, the man of the match, beat three defenders in a rousing run before crossing accurately for Goodfellow to head home.

It was an excellent work out for Thirds and an opportunity for the Israelis to gauge their playing standards in this their first match of their UK tour.

Thirds: Robertson; McGillivray, Caldwell; Reilly, McCormack, Cunningham; Goodfellow, McCool, Harley, Gray, McInnes.

Thirds 1 Rouen 2; Friendship Cup, 1st leg; 7th November, 1961.

This was Thirds' first taste of continental football and it proved to be quite a disaster. The weather was extremely unkind and, just an hour before the start, a downpour reduced the attendance to a mere 2,500.

The prevailing conditions, however, did not seem to upset the French team, playing in the Thirds' "red" whilst the Cathkin side adopted an all-black outfit to match the conditions.

Rouen attacked from the kick-off and only some desperate defending kept them out. Thirds seemed happy to hit on the break and, when they did, caused panic in the visiting defence. It took a magnificent save from French keeper Manolias to prevent a Goodfellow rocket from opening their account. Seconds later Alex Harley splashed his way through pools of water before being stopped inside the penalty area.

Rouen opened the scoring in 18 minutes with a real beauty. Buron dispossessed McGillivray on the left and swung over a low ball. Robelle met the cross first-time to beat Robertson with a vicious drive.

Thirds then went on all-out attack but keeper Manolias was in tremendous form. On three occasions, twice from Harley and then from a Gray header, the Frenchman saved his side.

Just after the break Thirds equalised. Jimmy Goodfellow crossed perfectly into the goalmouth and Rouen's Meyer deflected the ball into his own net.

Again the magnificent Manolias kept Thirds at bay with more super saves and a Rouen breakaway saw them grab the winner.

Thirds: Robertson; McGillivray, Caldwell; Robb, McCormack, Lewis; Goodfellow, Hilley, Harley, Gray, Fletcher.

Rouen 2 Thirds 1; Friendship Cup, 2nd Leg; 9th May, 1962.

Thirds: Robertson; McGillivray, Lewis; Reilly, McCormack, Cunningham; Goodfellow, Hilley, Harley, Gray, Fletcher. (Robb substituted for Reilly in second half).

Thirds took their second defeat from the Frenchmen on another rain-soaked pitch before a miserable attendance of only 2,000.

Thirds, however, had absolutely no luck and certainly were not favoured by the French referee, who allowed a series of jersey-pulling offences by Rouen players to go unpunished and repeatedly gave decisions in their favour. The Cathkin side were a goal behind in 39 minutes when slack defending allowed right-winger Cordel to hit home unchallenged. Willie Cunningham equalised for Thirds on the resumption with a cracking close-range shot, but, almost immediately, the Frenchmen went ahead again through Buron.

Manager George Young, following the game, was scathing in his comments, particularly about the quite apparent disinterest in this type of contest. The two games home and away had drawn only 4,500 fans.

Thirds were left to count the cost of their first European venture and, as it turned out, their last!

Celtic 1 Thirds 2; Glasgow Cup, Final; 8th April, 1963.

Robertson; McGillivray, Davis; Reilly, Lewis, Baird; Goodfellow, Spence, Cunningham, McMorran, McInnes.

The scene seemed set for another Celtic victory with Thirds having had an indifferent season but, under the captaincy of Sammy Baird (ex Rangers), the Hi Hi shocked all concerned with a resilient, determined and enthusiastic display.

It appeared that no-one fancied Thirds - including their "boss" Bill Hiddleston. It was reported that, in the dressing room just prior to kick-off, Hiddleston told his players: "There's £25 bonus per man to win the cup but I know you've no chance!" Some would call it perhaps obverse psychology, but the players simply went out and beat Celtic, although having to wait until the following week to receive their hard-earned bonus! Thirds were bidding to win the cup for the first time since 1909 and started the game in aggressive style. It took them only 10 minutes to shock Celtic with a glorious goal. Joe McInnes, cracked home a great volley from a Spence pass, to the delight of the Thirds fans.

Celtic equalised but, late on, Spence scored the winner when he took a defence-splitting McInnes pass in his stride to beat the Celts keeper.

A great night for Thirds ended with Sammy Baird being carried round Hampden shoulder-high displaying the trophy.

Celtic 4 Thirds 4; League; 14th September, 1963.

This was an ordinary league game with a difference. What Cathkin fan will ever forget the most amazing fight-back ever witnessed in a Thirds and Celtic clash?

Thirds: Mitchell; McGillivray, Davis; Dickson, Lewis, McLeod; Graham, Anderson, Cunningham, McMorran, Buckley.

Most fans will forgive players' faults providing they have plenty of fighting spirit and Thirds were certainly well endowed with that commodity in this memorable match.

No-one would have given a hoot for their chances as Celtic easily built up a four-goal lead in the opening 25 minutes. Turner, Lennox, Divers and Brogan delighted the Celtic crowd with well-taken goals. The few Thirds fans in attendance could hardly believe their eyes when Johnny Anderson hit a glorious double, quickly followed by a goal from young Paddy Buckley to put Thirds in with a chance just prior to the break.

When the Hi Hi had the temerity to equalise mid-way through the second half, with Graham the scorer, the home crowd were stunned. What would have happened had another two close efforts from Cunningham and McMorran gone in is anyone's guess. In the event a 4-4 draw it was, and the valuable point went to the fighting Thirds.

Nuneaton 1 Thirds 2; Thirds' last friendly; 6th August 1966

Thirds: Russell; Connell, Little; Harvey, Baillie, Stewart; McKay, Henderson, Fyfe, Kilgannon and Kinnaird. Second-half substitutes were May for Baillie, and McLaughlin for Kinnaird.

Seven minutes from time a cute Henderson lob beat the home 'keeper, to spare Thirds blushes, following a very indifferent performance. Henderson's goal was just about the game's highlight, with the leading-up work being exceptionally good. Little passed a fine ball to McKay, who touched it on to McLaughlin. Kilgannon, then took Mac's slick pass in his stride before releasing the ball to Henderson, whose well-judged lob hit the net.

Thirds started in the driving seat and gave home custodian Crump several early opportunities to shine. McKay and Stewart were linking well in midfield and, as a result of their leading-up work, Thirds opened the scoring in 25 minutes when Fyfe rose to meet a McKay cross and beat Crump easily.

Russell was then brought into things, and saved twice in quick succession to thwart eager home attacks.

Nuneaton equalised in 50 minutes through Crawley, and this shocked the visitors who ultimately regained enough composure to win through.

Thirds 3 Queen of the South 3; Last home game; Wednesday 26th April, 1967.

Thirds: Russell, Connell, Heaney; McLaughlin, Little, McEwan; Rundell, Craig, Busby, Kinnaird, Stewart.

A second-half revival by Queens that at one time never looked possible brought them a deserved point.

Thirds had trooped off at the interval with a comfortable 3-1 lead, but two goals from McMurdo, in a five-minute second-half spell, shocked the Cathkin boys.

Kinnaird opened for Thirds direct from a corner kick, and 20 minutes later McLaughlin made it 2-0 from a clever Stewart pass.

Davidson pulled one back for the Dumfries lads, but almost immediately Kinnaird put the Warriors two-up with a vicious volley.

Then came the McMurdo double. Thirds were struggling and ultimately glad of a share of the points.

Dumbarton 5 Thirds 1; Boghead Park; Last game; 28th April 1967.

The eleven men to don the scarlet for the last competitive game were: Russell; Connell, Heaney; McLaughlin, Little, McEwan; Rundell, Craig, Busby, May, Kinnaird.

Thirds were a goal down before a Hi Hi man had touched the ball. Dumbarton kicked off and scored within thirty seconds, McCormick doing the damage.

McMillan and Kirk brought the Sons' tally to three before the interval, and late on McLauglin and Kirk completed the rout, before Busby scored

Thirds' consolation counter, which put his name into the record books of Scottish football.

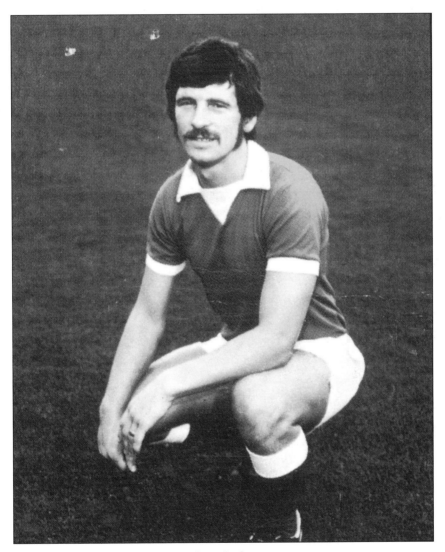

Drew Busby.

CHAPTER 7

SCORELINES

In all matches Third Lanark scores are recorded first.

Season 1939/40

League:

Home		Away
2-1	Hamilton Academical	0-4
3-2	Kilmarnock	1-0
1-2	Rangers	2-2
2-2	Albion Rovers	0-2
3-1	Morton	2-3
0-1	Queen of the South	3-6
1-1	Motherwell	2-6
1-4	Airdrie	1-2
4-2	Celtic	2-1
1-1	Ayr United	4-2
2-1	St Mirren	3-5
2-0	Partick Thistle	1-4
3-2	Dumbarton	1-3
3-0	Queen's Park	4-3
2-4	Clyde	1-0

Glasgow Charity Cup:

Celtic 3 Thirds 2

Glasgow Cup:

1st Round: Clyde 0 Thirds 1
Semi-Finals: Rangers 2 Thirds 2
Replay: Rangers 2 Thirds 1 (Ibrox)

Season 1940/41

Southern League Cup:

Home		Away
4-2	Dumbarton	0-0
1-2	Falkirk	2-2
1-2	Rangers	0-3

League:

Home		Away
0-3	Albion Rovers	0-6
3-4	Hamilton Academical	1-1
4-1	Dumbarton	4-6
0-3	Queen's Park	2-2
2-0	Hearts	2-4
1-6	Clyde	3-3
1-1	Motherwell	0-3
3-2	Airdrie	4-3
3-2	Hibernian	2-2
0-4	Falkirk	0-5
0-0	Partick Thistle	3-2
1-0	Celtic	3-4
2-2	Morton	1-4
0-1	Rangers	3-0
5-3	St Mirren	2-3

Glasgow Charity Cup:
Semi-Finals: Rangers 3 Thirds 2

Summer Cup:

Home		Away
5-2	Albion Rovers	4-1
0-1	Dumbarton	0-4

Season 1941/42

Southern League Cup:
Home		Away
3-5	Hearts	0-3
2-5	Rangers	1-5
1-1	Motherwell	1-1

League:
Home		Away
4-3	Dumbarton	5-1
5-3	Clyde	4-5
6-4	Hearts	5-1
4-1	Queen's Park	2-1
0-2	Rangers	1-6
4-4	Morton	2-3
3-4	Albion Rovers	3-1
4-2	Hibernian	0-6
0-3	Falkirk	2-3
3-2	Partick Thistle	2-2
2-1	St Mirren	0-4
1-1	Celtic	1-3
0-4	Motherwell	3-5
2-0	Airdrie	4-3
3-1	Hamilton Academical	4-3

Glasgow Charity Cup:
Celtic 2 Thirds 0

Summer Cup:
Home		Away
4-3	Airdrie	4-1
1-5	Hibernian	2-8

Season 1942/43

Southern League Cup:

Home		Away
2-0	Motherwell	2-2
3-2	Partick Thistle	1-1
5-1	Airdrie	3-1
	Semi-Finals: Falkirk 1-3	

League:

Home		Away
1-2	Clyde	0-2
1-2	Hearts	1-3
2-2	Morton	2-6
0-3	Rangers	2-4
3-2	Queen's Park	2-0
1-3	Albion Rovers	2-2
3-2	Hibernian	1-5
4-1	Falkirk	1-2
3-4	St Mirren	2-2
4-2	Celtic	2-3
2-0	Motherwell	2-5
1-0	Airdrie	0-4
1-2	Hamilton Academical	2-4
1-1	Partick Thistle	1-2
7-3	Dumbarton	3-5

Glasgow Charity Cup:
Semi-Finals: Partick Thistle 2 Thirds 3
Final: Celtic 3 Thirds 0

Summer Cup:

Home		Away
1-3	St Mirren	3-6

Season 1943/44

Southern League Cup:

Home		Away
0-4	Hibernian	0-4
0-5	Morton	1-2
2-2	Albion Rovers	2-4

League:

Home		Away
3-2	Albion Rovers	3-1
2-3	Dumbarton	3-2
1-2	Hearts	3-6
3-3	Queen's Park	1-4
7-2	Clyde	0-2
0-6	Rangers	1-3
4-3	Morton	1-2
3-2	Hamilton Academical	2-6
1-1	St Mirren	1-2
3-4	Motherwell	2-5
0-2	Hibernian	0-6
1-3	Falkirk	6-5
2-3	Airdrie	0-2
0-3	Partick Thistle	1-6
3-4	Celtic	0-0

Glasgow Cup:

Thirds 4 Queen's Park 3
Thirds 2 Partick Thistle 4

Summer Cup:

Home		Away
2-3	Partick Thistle	1-3

Season 1944/45

Southern League Cup:

Home		Away
2-1	Hibernian	1-3
3-3	Albion Rovers	3-2
2-4	Rangers	0-2

League:

Home		Away
0-1	Clyde	1-2
2-3	Morton	1-3
2-1	Hamilton Academical	2-5
1-2	Celtic	0-1
1-4	Rangers	0-0
2-0	Queen's Park	1-2
1-2	Hearts	1-4
2-1	Albion Rovers	0-1
0-2	Dumbarton	5-2
1-2	St Mirren	0-0
3-5	Airdrie	0-0
1-1	Motherwell	6-4
3-4	Hibernian	4-2
2-1	Falkirk	1-3
4-1	Partick Thistle	6-2

Summer Cup:

Home		Away
2-1	Falkirk	0-5

Glasgow Charity Cup:

Celtic 5 Thirds 0

Glasgow Cup:

Thirds 1 Celtic 2

Season 1945/46

League Cup:

Home		Away
1-0	Clyde	3-7
2-2	Queen's Park	4-1
0-4	Celtic	1-1

League:

Home		Away
3-1	Aberdeen	0-3
5-1	Queen of the South	3-5
1-2	Hearts	1-2
1-0	Queen's Park	1-1
1-5	Rangers	0-1
2-1	Morton	4-4
7-2	Hamilton Academical	1-0
3-1	St Mirren	4-3
0-2	Celtic	2-3
4-2	Partick Thistle	2-6
2-1	Hibernian	0-4
2-3	Falkirk	1-3
4-1	Kilmarnock	3-1
0-2	Motherwell	3-1
1-6	Clyde	2-1

Victory Cup:

1st Round: Thirds 1 Dunfermline 1
Dunfermline 0 Thirds 2
2nd Round: Falkirk 3 Thirds 2

Glasgow Charity Cup:

Semi-Finals: Partick Thistle 0 Thirds 1
Final: Rangers   2 Thirds 0
(Hampden Park - Attendance 48,700)

Glasgow Cup:

Thirds 1 Partick Thistle 2

Season 1946/47

League:

Home		Away
0-3	Aberdeen	0-1
1-1	Queen of the South	1-4
4-1	Hearts	1-4
1-4	Morton	0-2
1-1	Rangers	1-8
4-1	Partick Thistle	1-3
0-0	Celtic	4-1
3-4	Queen's Park	0-0
2-1	Hamilton Academical	2-2
0-2	Hibernian	1-4
4-2	Falkirk	2-2
5-1	St Mirren	4-2
1-4	Kilmarnock	2-0
2-1	Motherwell	1-2
5-3	Clyde	3-0

Scottish Cup:

> 1st Round: Hamilton Academical 1 Thirds 1
> Replay: Thirds 2 Hamilton Academical 1
> 2nd Round: Bye
> 3rd Round: Dumbarton 2 Thirds 0

League Cup:

Home		Away
2-3	Celtic	0-0
1-2	Hibernian	2-1
3-5	Hamilton Academical	0-3

Glasgow Charity Cup:

> Semi-Final: Celtic 1 Thirds 1
> (Celtic won on Corners 7-2)

Glasgow Cup:

> Semi-Finals: Partick Thistle 2 Thirds 3
> Final: Thirds 1 Clyde 2

179

Season 1947/48

League Cup:
Home		Away
5-1	Dundee	0-5
3-2	Celtic	1-3
1-3	Rangers	0-3

League:
Home		Away
2-2	Airdrie	1-2
3-2	Aberdeen	2-2
5-1	Celtic	3-1
2-1	Clyde	1-1
1-4	Dundee	2-5
2-0	Falkirk	1-8
4-1	Hearts	3-1
1-4	Hibernian	0-8
2-1	Morton	2-2
0-3	Motherwell	1-2
1-2	Partick Thistle	2-2
4-2	Queen's Park	2-2
5-1	Queen of the South	1-2
0-1	Rangers	2-5
1-4	St Mirren	0-1

Season 1948/49

League Cup:
Home		Away
1-1	Aberdeen	4-2
4-2	St Mirren	0-4
2-2	Morton	1-2

League:

Home		Away
2-1	Rangers	1-2
2-3	Dundee	1-1
3-2	Hibernian	0-1
2-2	East Fife	0-4
3-2	Falkirk	1-5
3-2	Celtic	2-1
1-1	Hearts	2-3
3-1	St Mirren	2-1
6-1	Queen of the South	1-2
1-2	Partick Thistle	3-1
1-3	Motherwell	0-1
1-0	Aberdeen	2-2
0-1	Clyde	0-2
1-0	Morton	3-3
4-1	Albion Rovers	5-1

Scottish Cup:

1st Round: Thirds 2 Aberdeen 1

2nd Round: Hearts 3 Thirds 1

Glasgow Charity Cup:

Celtic 2 Thirds 0

Glasgow Cup:

Semi-Final: Thirds 4 Rangers 1

Final: Celtic 3 Thirds 1

Season 1949/50

League Cup:

Home		Away
0-2	Hibernian	2-4
3-0	Falkirk	2-1
1-1	Queen of the South	4-2

League:

Home		Away
2-2	Rangers	1-3
0-2	Hibernian	1-0
3-0	Hearts	0-1
4-1	East Fife	1-3
1-0	Celtic	1-2
1-0	Dundee	4-1
2-7	Partick Thistle	1-5
3-1	Aberdeen	1-2
0-1	Raith Rovers	1-1
3-3	Motherwell	0-4
2-1	St Mirren	1-6
1-3	Clyde	2-0
0-2	Falkirk	1-2
2-1	Queen of the South	1-4
2-4	Stirling Albion	2-0

Scottish Cup:

1st Round: Thirds 2 Arbroath 1
2nd Round: Thirds 1 Celtic 1
Replay: Celtic 4 Thirds 1

Glasgow Charity Cup:

Celtic 1 Thirds 0

Glasgow Cup:

Thirds 4 Partick Thistle 2
Clyde 2 Thirds 2
Thirds 1 Clyde 4 (Replay)

Season 1950/51

League Cup:

Home		Away
1-0	Raith Rovers	2-3
1-2	Celtic	1-3
3-3	East Fife	5-2

League:

Home		Away
2-0	Motherwell	1-4
1-2	Raith Rovers	0-4
2-1	Falkirk	0-2
1-2	Clyde	2-0
0-2	Morton	3-1
1-5	Rangers	1-2
1-0	Airdrie	1-2
1-1	East Fife	1-3
2-0	Aberdeen	2-1
1-2	Hearts	0-4
2-0	Dundee	1-2
2-0	Celtic	1-1
1-2	St Mirren	4-0
1-2	Hibernian	1-3
4-2	Partick Thistle	0-1

Scottish Cup:

1st Round: Thirds 5 Forfar 2

2nd Round: Aberdeen 4 Thirds 0

Glasgow Charity Cup:

Semi-Finals: Rangers 1 Thirds 1

(Rangers won on toss of coin)

Glasgow Cup:

Thirds 2 Partick Thistle 2

Partick Thistle 4 Thirds 1

Season 1951/52

League Cup:

Home		Away
0-1	Celtic	1-1
2-0	Morton	2-5
5-0	Airdrie	1-2

183

League:

Home		Away
4-0	Airdrie	4-2
2-1	Queen of the South	0-1
0-0	Partick Thistle	2-4
0-5	Hibernian	2-5
4-2	St Mirren	0-3
1-3	East Fife	2-3
2-0	Aberdeen	3-2
4-0	Hearts	2-2
3-3	Celtic	2-2
3-1	Morton	1-3
0-1	Motherwell	1-1
1-1	Rangers	1-1
3-1	Raith Rovers	0-1
1-3	Stirling Albion	3-3
0-2	Dundee	0-6

Scottish Cup:

1st Round: Celtic 0 Thirds 0
Replay: Thirds 2 Celtic 1
2nd Round: Hamilton Academical 1 Thirds 1
Replay: Thirds 4 Hamilton Academical 0
3rd Round: Albion Rovers 1 Thirds 3
4th Round: Thirds 1 Falkirk 0
Semi-Final: Dundee 2 Thirds 0 (Easter Road)

Glasgow Charity Cup:

Semi-Final: Thirds 1 Rangers 0
Final: Thirds 2 Clyde 2
(Cup shared six months to each Club)

Glasgow Cup:

1st Round: Partick Thistle 0 Thirds 1
Semi-Final: Celtic 5 Thirds 2

Season 1952/53

League Cup:

Home		Away
2-4	Falkirk	1-2
3-1	Queen of the South	3-0
2-0	East Fife	1-0
0-2	Quarter-Final: Rangers	0-0

League:

Home		Away
2-3	Hearts	3-3
1-1	Falkirk	1-5
0-2	Rangers	1-4
5-0	Queen of the South	1-3
0-1	Aberdeen	3-4
1-2	Motherwell	5-1
2-1	Raith Rovers	4-3
2-0	Hibernian	1-7
1-3	Celtic	4-5
4-3	St Mirren	0-1
0-0	Dundee	0-3
2-1	Airdrie	2-4
0-3	East Fife	1-3
3-1	Partick Thistle	0-0
1-3	Clyde	2-5

Scottish Cup:

1st Round: Elgin City 2 Thirds 3
2nd Round: Wigtown 1 Thirds 3
* 3rd Round: Thirds 1 Hamilton Academical 0
4th Round: Clyde 1 Thirds 2
Semi-Final: Aberdeen 1 Thirds 1 (Ibrox)
Replay: Aberdeen 2 Thirds 1 (Ibrox)
* Attendance 26,234

Glasgow Charity Cup:
Semi-Final: Celtic 1 Thirds 1
(Celtic into Final on toss of coin)

Glasgow Cup:
Semi-Final: Partick Thistle 4 Thirds 2

Season 1953/54

League Cup:

Home		Away
3-1	Alloa Athletic	10-0
2-0	St Johnstone	1-4
7-0	Cowdenbeath	2-4
0-4	Quarter-Final: Hibernian	0-4

League:

Home		Away
1-0	Albion Rovers	0-1
0 1	Queen's Park	1-1
9-1	Dundee United	1-1
3-3	Alloa Athletic	4-1
3-7	Morton	3-0
9-2	St Johnstone	1-6
2-0	Kilmarnock	1-1
4-1	Cowdenbeath	3-1
1-2	Motherwell	1-1
2-2	Arbroath	2-2
1-1	Stenhousemuir	3-5
2-1	Dumbarton	2-3
3-0	Forfar Athletic	4-1
1-1	Dunfermline	3-0
2-2	Ayr United	6-0

Scottish Cup:
1st Round: Thirds 2 Stenhousemuir 2
Replay: Stenhousemuir 0 Thirds 0
2nd Replay: Thirds 1 Stenhousemuir 0 (Ibrox)
2nd Round: Thirds 7 Deveronvale 2
3rd Round: Thirds 0 Rangers 0
Replay: Rangers 4 Thirds 4
2nd Replay: Rangers 3 Thirds 2 (Ibrox)

Glasgow Charity Cup:
1st Round: Thirds 2 Clyde 2 (Thirds won by toss of coin)
Semi-Final: Thirds 1 Partick Thistle 1 (Thirds won by toss of coin)
Final: Thirds 1 Rangers 0

Glasgow Cup:
Semi-Final: Thirds 2 Partick Thistle 1
Final: Rangers 3 Thirds 0

Season 1954/55

League Cup:
Home		Away
4-0	Cowdenbeath	0-1
2-0	Queen's Park	2-1
1-2	Airdrie	0-2

League:
Home		Away
4-1	Morton	2-2
3-1	Queen's Park	1-3
2-0	Dundee United	0-2
2-0	Alloa Athletic	3-1
1-1	Hamilton Academical	1-5
2-1	Dunfermline	0-0
1-2	Albion Rovers	1-1
4-1	Forfar Athletic	3-3
0-2	Stenhousemuir	2-2

3-4	Airdrie	1-1
1-2	St Johnstone	3-1
2-1	Cowdenbeath	4-2
9-0	Ayr United	0-2
4-2	Brechin City	1-2
3-2	Arbroath	0-2

Scottish Cup:

2nd Round: Thirds 2 Queen of the South 1
3rd Round: Thirds 1 Motherwell 3

Glasgow Charity Cup:

Rangers 3 Thirds 1

Glasgow Cup:

Thirds 0 Rangers 2

Season 1955/56

League Cup:

Home		Away
1-4	Brechin City	1-2
1-0	Morton	0-2
3-0	Stenhousemuir	1-1

League:

Home		Away
9-0	Montrose	0-2
2-1	St Johnstone	0-2
5-2	Stenhousemuir	1-1
1-2	Brechin City	1-3
0-2	Queen's Park	1-3
3-2	Ayr United	0-1
6-1	Hamilton Academical	3-1
0-1	Dundee United	0-1
1-3	East Stirling	4-1
3-3	Berwick Rangers	1-3

4-0	Morton	1-6
0-0	Forfar Athletic	1-3
1-5	Cowdenbeath	4-1
1-0	Dumbarton	3-2
2-0	Alloa Athletic	4-2
2-1	Arbroath	0-1
6-2	Stranraer	2-4
7-0	Albion Rovers	1-2

Scottish Cup:

5th Round: St Mirren 6 Thirds 0

Glasgow Charity Cup:

Semi-Final: Thirds 1 Rangers 1 (Thirds won by toss of coin)
Final: Thirds 4 Partick Thistle 2

Glasgow Cup:

Semi-Final: Rangers 6 Thirds 0

Season 1956/57

League Cup:

Home		Away
8-2	Stenhousemuir	1-2
1-5	Ayr United	3-3
1-2	Dundee United	1-2

League:

Home		Away
3-2	Cowdenbeath	4-3
4-3	Alloa Athletic	1-1
1-3	Clyde	1-2
6-1	Forfar Athletic	1-2
6-1	Montrose	1-1
7-0	Dumbarton	1-0
2-3	Dundee United	1-0
5-2	East Stirling	4 1

1-2	St Johnstone	6-3
3-0	Stranraer	0-2
3-0	Hamilton Academical	1-1
7-0	Stenhousemuir	3-2
5-1	Brechin City	3-1
5-1	Morton	5-1
3-0	Arbroath	0-2
1-0	Stirling Albion	0-3
4-0	Albion Rovers	0-5
2-0	Berwick Rangers	5-2

Scottish Cup:

Dundee United 5 Thirds 2

Glasgow Charity Cup:

Partick Thistle 1 Thirds 1 (Thirds into Semi-Final by toss of coin)
Semi-Final: Thirds 1 Queen's Park 4

Glasgow Cup:

Clyde 2 Thirds 2
Thirds 0 Clyde   0
Clyde 4 Thirds 2

Season 1957/58

League Cup:

Home		Away
3-0	Stenhousemuir	3-3
1-0	Morton	3-3
2-0	Stirling Albion	1-0
0-3	Quarter-Final: Celtic	1-6

League:

Home		Away
2-0	Raith Rovers	2-4
1-3	Queen's Park	3-1
3-5	Falkirk	2-4

2-1	Kilmarnock	4-2
0-0	Hearts	2-7
3-1	Airdrie	3-2
0-2	Celtic	1-4
1-4	Partick Thistle	3-2
5-1	Dundee	0-2
3-1	Aberdeen	4-2
1-2	East Fife	6-0
1-3	St Mirren	2-2
1-1	Hibernian	0-4
2-3	Queen of the South	1-6
1-5	Rangers	1-5
4-2	Motherwell	2-1
2-5	Clyde	1-1

Scottish Cup:
1st Round: Chirnside United 0 Thirds 4
2nd Round: Thirds 6 Lossiemouth 1
3rd Round: Thirds 5 Queen's Park 3
4th Round: Hibernian 3 Thirds 2

Glasgow Charity Cup:
1st Round: Thirds 1 Queen's Park 3

Glasgow Cup:

Semi-Final: Thirds 2 Queen's Park 2
Replay: Queen's Park 1 Thirds 3
Final: Thirds 1 Rangers 1
Replay: Rangers 4 Thirds 2

Season 1958/59

League Cup:

Home		Away
4-2	Raith Rovers	1-3
4-5	Hearts	0-3
0-3	Rangers	2-2

League:

Home		Away
2-3	Rangers	2-2
7-1	Queen of the South	5-2
2-2	Clyde	2-1
0-2	Aberdeen	3-3
0-4	Hearts	3-8
3-2	Raith Rovers	4-2
5-2	Motherwell	1-8
3-0	Stirling Albion	3-2
1-1	Celtic	1-3
0-1	Partick Thistle	1-1
2-2	Hibernian	4-4
1-1	Airdrie	1-1
0-3	Dundee	0-3
7-1	Dunfermline	3-2
3-3	Falkirk	0-2
2-3	St Mirren	1-4
2-0	Kilmarnock	0-4

Scottish Cup:

2nd Round: Dundee United 0 Thirds 4
3rd Round: Thirds 3 Alloa 2
Quarter-Finals: Thirds 2 Hibernian 1
Semi-Finals: Thirds 1 Aberdeen 1 (Ibrox)
Replay: Thirds 0 Aberdeen 1 (Ibrox)

Glasgow Charity Cup:

1st Round: Thirds 1 Clyde 3

Glasgow Cup:

1st Round: Celtic 2 Thirds 4
Semi-Final: Thirds 1 Rangers 2

Season 1959/60

League Cup:

Home		Away
2-0	Clyde	2-2
6-1	Dunfermline	3-2
3-1	St Mirren	3-2
2-1	Quarter-Finals: Falkirk	3-0

Semi-Finals: Thirds 3 Arbroath 0 (Ibrox)
Final: Hearts 2 Thirds 1

League:

Home		Away
2-2	St Mirren	3-1
5-0	Ayr United	3-2
1-2	Partick Thistle	0-2
5-3	Hibernian	0-6
2-0	Dunfermline	1-3
4-2	Airdrie	2-3
1-4	Hearts	2-6
1-3	Raith Rovers	3-2
3-4	Kilmarnock	2-3
2-1	Aberdeen	1-3
1-4	Motherwell	3-3
7-1	Arbroath	1-2
2-3	Clyde	3-2
0-2	Rangers	2-1
2-2	Dundee	1-2
4-2	Celtic	0-4
3-3	Stirling Albion	3-0

Scottish Cup:

Clyde 2 Thirds 0

Glasgow Cup:

1st Round: Thirds 0 Clyde 2

Glasgow Charity Cup:

Thirds 3 Queen's Park 0
Semi-Finals: Partick Thistle 3 Thirds 2

Season 1960/61

League Cup:

Home		Away
1-3	Celtic	0-2
3-1	Partick Thistle	4-0
2-1	Rangers	2-3

League:

Home		Away
5-2	Airdrie	1-4
3-3	Ayr United	3-2
2-0	Celtic	3-2
1-2	St Mirren	0-1
2-4	Rangers	3- 4
5-1	Aberdeen	3-5
1-1	Motherwell	5-4
4-2	Dunfermline	3-2
0-1	Kilmarnock	1-3
6-1	Dundee United	2-1
2-1	Dundee	2-0
4-3	Raith Rovers	6-3
7-4	Clyde	4-2
0-3	Hearts	0-1
3-2	Partick Thistle	1-2
4-2	St Johnstone	4-3
6-1	Hibernian	4-8

Scottish Cup:

1st Round: Thirds 2 Stenhousemuir 0
2nd Round: Thirds 5 Arbroath 2
3rd Round: St. Mirren 3 Thirds 3
Replay: Thirds 0 St Mirren 8

Glasgow Charity Cup:

Thirds 5 Partick Thistle 2
Thirds 1 Clyde 2

Glasgow Cup:

Thirds 0 Celtic 0
Celtic 3 Thirds 1

Season 1961/62

League Cup:

Home		Away
0-2	Rangers	0-5
3-2	Dundee	2-2
3-1	Airdrie	2-2

League:

Home		Away
3-0	Airdrie	2-0
1-1	Celtic	0-1
4-2	Partick Thistle	0-2
1-1	Stirling Albion	0-2
1-3	Dundee	1-2
7-2	Dundee United	0-3
3-1	Kilmarnock	2-2
2-1	Raith Rovers	3-4
1-2	Hibernian	3-1
0-3	Rangers	1-3
3-5	Aberdeen	1-2
1-0	Hearts	1-2
2-1	Motherwell	3-0
1-1	Dunfermline	1-1
5-2	St Mirren	2-1
1-2	St Johnstone	2-1
1-4	Falkirk	0-2

British - Franco Cup:

Home		Away
1-2	Rouen	1-2

Scottish Cup:
1st Round: Berwick Rangers 2 Thirds 6
2nd Round: Hamilton Academical 0 Thirds 2
3rd Round: Thirds 6 Inverness Caley 1
4th Round: Celtic 4 Thirds 4
Replay: Thirds 0 Celtic 4 (Hampden)

Glasgow Cup:
Home		Away
1-1	Clyde	5-2
		(Replay)
4-1	Rangers	
1-1	Celtic	2-3
		(Replay)

Season 1962/63

League Cup:
Home		Away
2-5	Rangers	2-5
1-4	Hibernian	2-3
1-2	St Mirren	1-1

League:
Home		Away
2-1	Raith Rovers	1-1
3-3	Falkirk	5-3
0-1	Kilmarnock	2-2
1-1	Dundee United	0-1
1-2	Aberdeen	1-4
2-2	Motherwell	3-3
4-0	Dunfermline	0-3
1-4	Rangers	0-1
2-1	Clyde	2-3
1-4	Hibernian	1-1
2-3	Airdrie	4-1
1-2	Hearts	0-2

4-3	Dundee	2-5
1-1	St Mirren	4-2
1-0	Queen of the South	1-2
2-0	Celtic	1-2
0-1	Partick Thistle	1-3

Scottish Cup:

1st Round: East Fife 1 Thirds 1
Replay: Thirds 1 East Fife 1
Replay: Thirds 2 East Fife 0
2nd Round: Thirds 0 Raith Rovers 1

Glasgow Cup:

Thirds 6 Queen's Park 3
Semi-Final: Thirds 0 Clyde 0
Replay: Clyde 2 Thirds 5
Final: Thirds 2 Celtic 1

Season 1963/64

League Cup:

Home		Away
2-1	Airdrie	3-2
1-2	Dundee	2-3
0-3	Dunfermline	3-2

League:

Home		Away
1-2	Aberdeen	1-1
1-2	Airdrie	0-1
1-1	Celtic	4-4
1-2	Dundee	0-6
2-2	Dundee United	1-4
0-1	Dunfermline	0-3
1-2	East Stirling	3-2
0-2	Hearts	1-4
3-7	Falkirk	2-2

1-0	Hibernian	0-3
1-2	Kilmarnock	0-2
3-1	Motherwell	1-1
3-2	Partick Thistle	1-0
1-1	Queen of the South	4-2
0-5	Rangers	1-2
4-2	St Mirren	0-1
4-2	St Johnstone	1-0

Scottish Cup:
1st Round: Stranraer 2 Thirds 1

Summer Cup:

Home		Away
1-3	Morton	1-1
4-2	Partick Thistle	2-7
1-2	St Mirren	0-1

Glasgow Cup:
Semi-Final: Celtic 1 Thirds 1
Replay: Thirds 0 Celtic 3

Season 1964/65

League Cup:

Home		Away
0-2	Hibernian	0-3
0-1	Dunfermline	1-3
5-2	Airdrie	2-1

League:

Home	Away	
0-4	Kilmarnock	1-3
1-2	Morton	0-4
0-2	Motherwell	3-3
1-5	Hearts	1-3
0-4	Clyde	0-1

4-1	Aberdeen	1-3
1-2	Dundee United	1-4
0-3	Partick Thistle	1-0
1-2	Falkirk	0-3
0-2	St Johnstone	0-5
0-4	Airdrie	1-2
0-2	Hibernian	0-5
2-1	St Mirren	1-2
0-3	Celtic	0-1
1-2	Dunfermline	0-8
0-1	Dundee	1-6
0-1	Rangers	0-5

Scottish Cup:
1st Round: Inverness Caley 1 Thirds 5
2nd Round: Thirds 1 Dunfermline 1
Replay: Dunfermline 2 Thirds 2
2nd Replay: Dunfermline 4 Thirds 2 (Tynecastle)

Summer Cup:
Home		Away
1-5	Motherwell	1-3
0-3	Kilmarnock	2-6
5-2	Airdrie	1-3

Glasgow Cup:
Queen's Park 2 Thirds 0

Season 1965/66

League Cup:
Home		Away
5-1	Hamilton Academical	2-2
3-2	Berwick Rangers	1-4
1-1	Cowdenbeath	1-0
1-2	Ayr United	0-1

(Play off for Quarter-Final)

League:

Home		Away
1-1	Ayr United	0-2
0-2	Airdrie	3-3
9-1	Forfar Athletic	2-1
0-2	East Stirling	3-2
1-0	Arbroath	2-5
0-0	Brechin	3-1
7-1	Alloa Athletic	0-3
4-1	East Fife	0-1
2-1	Albion Rovers	1-1
1-0	Raith Rovers	1-6
1-2	Montrose	0-3
1-0	Cowdenbeath	3-3
0-2	Queen's Park	2-0
1-1	Queen of the South	1-4
1-1	Berwick Rangers	0-4
2-1	Stranraer	1-2
0-2	Dumbarton	1-3
1-1	Stenhousemuir	0-2

Scottish Cup:

1st Round: Hibernian 4 Thirds 3

Glasgow Cup:

1st Round: Partick Thistle 0 Thirds 1
(The competition was declared void for this season)

Season 1966/67

League Cup:

Home		Away
1-1	Arbroath	0-2
0-1	Morton	2-3
2-3	East Fife	2-2

League:

Home		Away
3-2	Hamilton Academical	1-1
2-0	Arbroath	1-2
4-3	Queen's Park	1-3
3-3	Queen of the South	2-3
1-1	Morton	0-6
1-6	Raith Rovers	1-4
3-0	Berwick Rangers	0-2
3-0	Alloa Athletic	0-1
7-4	Montrose	1-4
6-2	Forfar Athletic	3-5
2-0	Albion Rovers	0-1
1-3	Stranraer	2-2
1-1	Cowdenbeath	1-2
3-2	East Fife	1-3
0-0	East Stirling	0-1
3-1	Stenhousemuir	2-0
1-1	Brechin City	3-3
1-0	Clydebank	2-0
0-1	Dumbarton	1-5

Scottish Cup:

2nd Preliminary Round: Brechin City 1 Thirds 0

Glasgow Cup:

1st Round: Thirds 2 Clyde 2
Replay: Clyde 3 Thirds 1

Season 1966/67
A complete breakdown of the final seasons statistics.

Goalscorers:

Henderson	13
Fyfe	12
Stewart	12
McLaughlin	11
J. Kilgannon	11
Busby	5
Kinnaird	4
Craig	1
May	1
Newman	1
McKay	1
McCallum	1
Harvey	1
Baillie	1
Small	1 og (Hamilton Academical)
Munro	1 og (Montrose)

Competition:	P	W	D	L	F	A	Points	Position
League	38	13	8	17	67	78	34	11th
League Cup	6	-	2	4	7	12	2	ko
Scottish Cup	1	-	-	1	-	1	-	ko
Glasgow Cup	2	-	1	1	3	5	-	ko
	47	13	11	23	77	96	36	

CHAPTER 8

GENERAL STATISTICS 1872-1967

Biggest Victory:
31st October 1885 Thirds 11 St Andrews 0, Scottish Cup 3rd Round.

Biggest Defeat:
1924/25 Thirds 0 Motherwell 8 Division 1.
1947/48 Thirds 0 Hibernian 8 Division 1.
1960/61 Thirds 0 St Mirren 8 Scottish Cup Replay.
1964/65 Dunfermline 8 Thirds 0 Division 1.

Most League Points:
1930/31 Division 2. 61 points.

Most League Goals:
1930/31 Division 2. 107 goals.

League Scoring Records:
1934/35 George Hay 46 (Second Division).
1960/61 Alex Harley 42 (First Division).

Most Capped Player:
James Brownlie, 16 full Scotland caps and 14 Scottish League honours.

First Capped Player:
John Hunter, 1874.

Biggest attendance at Cathkin:
February 1954 v Rangers Scottish Cup 3rd Round 45,455.

Lowest attendance at Cathkin:
April 1967 v Clydebank 297.

Honours:

League Winners:
Champions Division 1 1903/04
Champions Division 2 1930/31 and 1934/35
Runners-Up Division 2 1927/28 and 1956/57

Scottish Cup:
Winners:
1889 v Celtic 2-1 After Replay (Oswald 2) Snow Final
1905 v Rangers 3-1 After Replay (Wilson 2 Johnstone)

Runners Up:
1876 v Queens Park
1878 v Vale of Leven
1906 v Hearts
1936 v Rangers

Scottish League Cup:
Runners Up 1959/60

Glasgow Cup:
Winners
1902/03
1903/04
1908/09
1962/63

Runners up
1890/91
1905/06
1906/07
1913/14
1923/24
1937/38
1942/43
1946/47
1947/48
1948/49
1953/54
1957/58

Glasgow Charity Cup:
Winners
1889/90
1897/98
1900/01

1951/52 (Shared with Clyde)
1953/54
1955/56

Runners Up
1883/84
1896/97
1909/10
1913/14
1931/32
1938/39
1942/43
1945/46

Most Successful Season:
1903/04 Winning Record 76.9%.

Best Goalscoring Record:
1892/93 Goals 54 average 3 per game Division 1.
1930/31 Goals 107 average 2.82 per game Division 2.
1956/57 Goals 105 average 2.91 per game Division 2.
1960/61 Goals 100 average 2.94 per game Division 1.

Worst Goalscoring Record:
1964/65 Goals 22 average 0.65 per game.

Best Defensive Record:
1903/04 Goals 26 average 1 per game.

Worst Defensive Record:
1964/65 Goals 99 average 2.91 per game.

Last major cup final:
24th October 1959 Hearts 2 Thirds 1 League Cup Final.

Last Cup Final:
8th April 1963 Thirds 2 Celtic 1 Glasgow Cup Final.

Unique Scoring Record:
Left winger Joe McInnes, scored five goals on his debut against
Stenhousemuir at Cathkin in a League Cup game on 11th August 1956.

Players Capped:
Full Scotland Caps:
J Brownlie
J Mason
J Carabine
J Auld
W Blair
J Cross
N Dewar
R Downie
J Fyfe
D Gardner
J Gillespie
J Hannah
D Hill
J Hunter
W Johnstone
A Kennedy
J McAdam
J Marshall
W Miller
J Oswald
J Rae
J Raeside
J Simpson
T Sloan
W Somers
A Stewart
A Thomson
F Walker
J Weir
H Wilson
T Smith
JH Cross
J Lang
A Lochhead
W McIntosh
R Mitchell

Scottish League Honours:
W Wardrope
J Warden
R Orr
W Porter
T Fairfoul
D Hilley
J Kelly
R Barbour
L Bell
J Blair
H Boyd
J Gillespie
A Thompson
J Carabine
R Mitchell

U 23 Caps:
D Hilley
F McGillivray

Club Managers:
1872: R Moodie (Secretary/Manager)
1885: J Thomson (Secretary/Manager)
1893: WA Abel (Secretary/Manager)
1910: M Tarbert
1919: R Moreland
1922: A Bennett
1925: M Richardson
1934: T Jennings
1939: G McMillan
1946: J Carabine
1949: A Ritchie
1954: J Blair
1955: W Hiddleston
1957: R Shankly
1959: G Young
1962: W Steel
1964: R Evans
1966: F Joyner
1967: R Shearer

First League goal scored:
Colonel John B Wilson September 1890.

Last League goal scored:
Drew Busby v Dumbarton April 28th 1967.

Third Lanark (Original members of the Scottish League)

Season	P	W	D	L	F	A	Pts	Division	Position
*1890/91	18	8	3	7	38	39	15	SL	5
1891/92	22	8	5	9	44	47	21	SL	6
1892/93	18	9	1	8	54	40	19	SL	4
1893/94	18	7	3	8	37	45	17	1	7
1894/95	18	10	1	7	51	39	21	1	4
1895/96	18	7	1	10	47	51	15	1	6
1896/97	18	5	1	12	29	46	11	1	8
1897/98	18	8	2	8	37	38	18	1	5
1898/99	18	7	3	8	33	38	17	1	6
1899/1900	18	5	5	8	31	37	15	1	7
1900/01	20	6	6	8	20	29	18	1	6
1901/02	18	7	5	6	30	26	19	1	4
1902/03	22	8	5	9	34	27	21	1	7
1903/04	26	20	3	3	61	26	43	1	1
1904/05	26	14	7	5	60	28	35	1	3
1905/06	30	16	2	12	62	39	34	1	6
1906/07	34	15	9	10	57	48	39	1	6

Season	P	W	D	L	F	A	Pts	Division	Position
1907/08	34	13	7	14	45	50	33	1	9
1908/09	34	11	10	13	56	49	32	1	11
1909/10	34	13	8	13	62	44	34	1	7
1910/11	34	16	7	11	59	53	39	1	8
1911/12	34	12	7	15	40	57	31	1	11
1912/13	34	8	12	14	31	41	28	1	15
1913/14	38	13	10	15	42	51	36	1	8
1914/15	38	10	12	16	51	57	32	A	16
1915/16	38	9	11	18	38	56	29	SL	17
1916/17	38	19	11	8	53	37	49	SL	5
1917/18	34	10	7	17	56	62	27	SL	13
1918/19	34	11	9	14	60	60	31	SL	12
+1919/20	41	16	11	14	56	61	43	SL	9
1920/21	42	19	6	17	74	61	44	SL	8
1921/22	42	17	12	13	58	52	46	1	9
1922/23	38	11	8	19	40	59	30	1	17
1923/24	38	11	8	19	54	78	30	1	18
1924/25	38	11	8	19	53	84	30	1	20
1925/26	38	19	8	11	72	47	46	2	6
1926/27	38	17	10	11	67	48	44	2	4
1927/28	38	18	9	11	99	66	45	2	2
1928/29	38	10	6	22	71	102	26	1	19

Season	P	W	D	L	F	A	Pts	Division	Position
1929/30	38	23	6	9	92	53	52	2	4
1930/31	38	27	7	4	107	42	61	2	1
1931/32	38	21	4	13	92	81	46	1	4
1932/33	38	14	7	17	70	80	35	1	13
1933/34	38	8	9	21	62	103	25	1	19
1934/35	34	23	6	5	94	43	52	2	1
1935/36	38	14	5	19	63	71	33	1	11
1936/37	38	20	6	12	79	61	46	1	6
1937/38	38	11	13	14	68	73	35	1	9
1938/39	38	12	8	18	80	96	32	1	15
1939/40 to 1945/46 Competition suspended									
1946/47	30	11	6	13	56	64	28	A	9
1947/48	30	10	6	14	56	73	26	A	11
1948/49	30	13	5	12	56	52	31	A	7
1949/50	30	11	3	16	44	62	25	A	12
1950/51	30	11	2	17	40	51	24	A	13
1951/52	30	9	8	13	51	62	26	A	12
1952/53	30	8	4	18	52	75	20	A	16
1953/54	30	13	10	7	78	48	36	B	3
1954/55	30	13	7	10	63	49	33	B	5
1955/56	36	16	3	17	80	64	35	B	10
1956/57	36	24	3	9	105	51	51	2	2

Season	P	W	D	L	F	A	Pts	Division	Position
1957/58	34	13	4	17	69	88	30	1	14
1958/59	34	11	10	13	74	83	32	1	11
1959/60	34	13	4	17	75	83	30	1	12
1960/61	34	20	2	12	100	80	42	1	3
1961/62	34	13	5	16	59	60	31	1	11
1962/63	34	9	8	17	56	68	26	1	14
1963/64	34	9	7	18	47	74	25	1	16
1964/65	34	3	1	30	22	99	7	1	18
1965/66	36	12	8	16	55	65	32	2	14
1966/67	38	13	8	17	67	78	34	2	11

Overall League Record (70 Seasons)
P. 2239 W. 882 D. 444 L. 913 F. 4074 A. 4050 PTS. 2204 Success Rate: 49.2%
* Four points deducted for rule infringements.
+ Only played Albion Rovers once.